IMAGES OF WOMEN

Report of the Task Force on
Sex-Role Stereotyping in
the Broadcast Media

La version française est aussi disponible

Available in Canada through authorized bookstore
agents and other bookstores or by mail from

Canadian Government Publishing Centre
Supply and Services Canada
Hull, Québec, Canada K1A 0S9

Catalogue No. BC92-26/1982E   Canada: $3.95
ISBN 0-660-90921-9   Other countries: $4.75

Price subject to change without notice.

LETTER OF TRANSMITTAL

Dr. John Meisel
Chairman
Canadian Radio-television and
  Telecommunications Commission
Ottawa, Ontario K1A 0N2

Dear Dr. Meisel:

We, the members of the Task Force on Sex-Role Stereotyping in the Broadcast Media, are pleased to submit the following report for consideration by the Commission.

Marianne Barrie
President

Marge Anthony

Camille Bachand

Stella Baudot

Edward Billo

Claude Blain

Maria Eriksen

Edythe Goodridge

Rosalie Gower

Jane Hughes

Louise Imbeàult

Suzanne Keeler

Beth Percival

Michael Kennerley

James Robson

Lynn McDonald

Sylvia Spring

Phillip Moyes

G.G.E. Steele

CONTENTS

APPENDICES

COMPOSITION OF THE TASK FORCE

CRTC Commissioners

Marianne Barrie (President of the Task Force)

Edythe Goodridge

Rosalie Gower

James Robson, who replaced R. MacLeod Rogers

Public Members

Stella Baudot, Montréal, Québec: specialist in public opinion surveys and social research, formerly with the Canadian Advisory Council on the Status of Women and former Vice-President of la Fédération des femmes du Québec

Maria Eriksen, Edmonton, Alberta: psychologist, founding member of the Alberta Status of Women Committee

Jane Hughes, Toronto, Ontario: editor, Homemaker's Magazine; also served as a member of the 1977 Canadian Advertising Advisory Board's Task Force on Women and Advertising

Lynn McDonald, Toronto, Ontario: sociologist and former President, National Action Committee on the Status of Women

Beth Percival, Charlottetown, P.E.I.: assistant professor of psychology, University of Prince Edward Island, and former president of the Canadian Research Institute for the Advancement of Women

Sylvia Spring, Galiano Island, B.C.: writer and director in media, founder of "Media Watch", and member, Vancouver Status of Women

CBC Representative

Louise Imbeault, Coordinator, Portrayal of Women in Programming, who replaced Dorienne Wilson-Smillie

Private Broadcasting Industry Representatives

Marge Anthony, Vice-President, Network Relations, CTV Network

Edward Billo, General Manager, CJOH-TV, television representative for the Canadian Association of Broadcasters

Claude Blain, Executive Vice-President, TVA Network. Jean-Paul Ladouceur served as a representative for the TVA Network from July 1980 to January 1982.

G.G.E. Steele, President, Canadian Association of Broadcasters, radio representative for the Canadian Association of Broadcasters, who replaced H. Paul Chamberland, CFCF Inc.

Advertising Industry Representatives

Camille Bachand, Vice-President, BCP Publicité Ltée, representative for the Publicité-Club de Montréal

Suzanne Keeler, Director, Public Affairs, Advertising Advisory Board

Michael Kennerley, Director, Media and Commercial Production, General Foods Inc., representative for the Association of Canadian Advertisers

Keith McKerracher, President, Institute of Canadian Advertising (resigned 7 February 1980)

Phillip Moyes, Executive Vice-President, Grocery Products Manufacturers of Canada, who replaced David Morley of the same association. (A representative of GPMC was invited to replace the ICA representative after his resignation.)

Ex-officio Members

Doris Anderson and Suzanne Findlay, Canadian Advisory Council on the Status of Women, during their tenure as officers of the council

FOREWORD

The Task Force on Sex-Role Stereotyping in the Broadcast Media wishes to call your attention to the following facts about women in Canada.

1. Women make up 51% of the population, age 15 and over. (April 1982)[1]

2. 50.3% of all women, age 15 and over, are in the labor force. (April 1982)[2]

3. There has been a 70.4% increase in the female labor force since 1970. (1981)[3]

4. 41.4% of employed Canadians are women. (April 1982)[4]

5. 43.5% of all women in the labor force solely support themselves, or themselves and others. (1979)[5]

6. 46.3% of all married women are employed outside the home. (April 1982)[6]

7. For every dollar a full-time male employee earns, a full-time female employee earns only 62.9 cents. (1979)[7]

8. 9.8% of all Canadian families are single parent families; 83% of these are headed by women. (1976)[8]

9. 57% of Canadian women are age 25 and over. (1979)[9]

PREFACE

It is not easy for nineteen people of such diverse back-grounds as ours to come to a meeting of minds on as complex an issue as sex-role stereotyping. Soon after we commenced our work it became evident that we all had brought varying perceptions of the dimensions of the problem to the table. We had a few stormy sessions, a resignation, and admittedly, some occasional feelings of mistrust. However, we worked through our problems, mediated our differences, and ended our discussions with pride on the part of all Task Force members in what is written here.

When we began in October 1979, we optimistically set as our goal the completion of the report within one year. Perhaps we could have met that goal if we had chosen merely to write a report suggesting solutions to industry, the government, and the CRTC. Instead, we opted to participate with industry in initiating change.

After considerable discussion, the Task Force agreed that broadcasters and advertisers be given the opportunity to demonstrate that self-regulation could achieve the results we were seeking. For the public members this was a compromise position undertaken with the understanding that it was to be for a two-year trial period. As we moved toward the concept of self-regulation as opposed to a regulatory code, industry began to react positively. Each segment developed action plans in consultation with Task Force members. As we write this document, many of their undertakings are already in place. We list these in Chapter 7 as "Achievements."

The final chapter of this report contains not only these achievements but also further recommendations which all members deem necessary if self-regulation is to work. In addition to these, the Task Force agreed that it was appropriate to have additional and specific recommendations from the public members included in this section.

This has been a Task Force like few others. Many positive steps toward the solution to the problem we were examining are already in place and some degree of change is becoming evident on the airwaves of the nation.

Marianne Barrie
President
Task Force on Sex-Role Stereotyping
in the Broadcast Media

ACKNOWLEDGEMENTS

The Task Force wishes especially to acknowledge the work of John Coleman, Louise Imbeault, Michael Kennerley, Beth Percival, and Sylvia Spring, who, with the President, formed the Task Force's Editorial Board. The board members took considerable time from their ongoing responsibilities to oversee the writing and production of this report.

As well, the Task Force would like to acknowledge the assistance of the following resource persons:

1. **From the advertising industry:**

Ken Barnes, President, Advertising Advisory Board (AAB)

Hugh Bonney, President, Norman, Craig & Kummel in Canada Ltd.

Evelyn Crandell, Director, Advertising Standards Council, and Chairman of its Children's Section

John Foss, President, Association of Canadian Advertisers (ACA)

Roger Godbeer, Director of Marketing Services, Colgate-Palmolive Canada, and Vice-Chairman, ACA

Susan Lenard, Vice-President, Scali, McCabe, Sloves Canada Ltd., and that company's representative to the Institute of Canadian Advertising (ICA)

Geoffrey Leonard, Managing Director, Vick Chemical Co., and that company's representative to the ACA

Bob Oliver, President, Advertising Standards Council

Robert Paquin, Advertising Manager, Johnson and Johnson Co. Ltd., and a Director of ACA

O.J. Reynolds, Advertising Consultant to the AAB

Shirley Slade, Media Manager, Carling O'Keefe Breweries of Canada Ltd., and Vice-Chairman of the ACA

Stephen Wilgar, President, Canada/Latin America Region, Warner-Lambert International

2. From the Broadcasting Industry

Gilles Brissette, former Assistant to the Director of Programming, French Services Division, CBC

Gordon Bruce, Vice-President, Corporate Affairs, English Services Division, CBC

John Coleman, Vice-President, Planning and Development, CTV (Although not formally a member of the Task Force, Mr. Coleman served on the Task Force Editorial Board.)

Jack Craine, Director of Television Programming, English Services Division, CBC

Fran Cutler, Executive Producer, English Services Division, CBC Radio

Helen Hutchinson, co-host, W-5 (CTV)

Lionel Lumb, former producer, W-5 (CTV)

Mark Lewis, former Associate Director, Government and Industry Relations, CTV

Helen McVey, Director, Office of Equal Opportunity, CBC

Pierre Nadeau, Vice-President, Government Relations and Public Policy, CAB

Jacqueline Pilote, Business Manager, CTV news, Features and Information Programming

Maxene Raices, Human Resources Development Officer, Ontario Educational Communications Authority (OECA)

Dodi Robb, Director for the Maritime Provinces, English Services Division, CBC

Deanna Rutherford, former Coordinator, Office of Equal Opportunity, CBC

Tony Scapillati, Legal Adviser, Government Relations and Public Policy, CAB

Phyllis Switzer, Vice-President, Programming and Public Relations, CITY-TV

The Task Force also wishes to express its appreciation to all corporations and associations from both the broadcasting and advertising industries that made the valuable services of their employees available to us.

3. Other Resource Persons

Andréa Martinez, former student, University of Montréal

Fabienne Mercier, former student, University of Montréal

The support staff for the Task Force was drawn from CRTC personnel augmented by three consultants who were involved with the writing and editing of this report. We were fortunate to have women and men with such a high degree of talent, ability, and dedication working with us on this project. We are grateful particularly to:

Andrée Wylie, CRTC legal counsel who acted as Secretary to the Task Force.

Ralph Hart, CRTC Senior Policy Adviser, who acted as Executive Staff Consultant to the Task Force.

Richard Frith, and his predecessor Ted Ledingham, coordinators of the overall work of the Task Force, both of whom had the awesome ability of coping efficiently with the myriad of details involved in the administration of a task force of this size. As well, Mr. Ledingham, prior to his leaving the CRTC, made a significant contribution to the writing and preparation of the Task Force report.

Leslie Wallace, Writing and Research Consultant, who succeeded in the difficult assignment of translating the varying views and perceptions of the Editorial Board into a cohesive document to which all 19 Task Force members could agree.

Brenda Fleet, Editorial Consultant, and Francine Fournier-Paluck, Consultant on the French Language, for their work in editing the report in both English and French.

Other CRTC staff members who made major contributions of time and effort in the fields of research and production of this report were:

Ninon Charlebois, translator, Secretary of State of Canada--CRTC

Claire DesLauriers-Leclair, secretarial support

Suzanne Dufour, secretarial support

Veronique Fiset, secretarial support

Lise Gauthier, secretarial support

Françoise Icart, research officer

Gail Jabour, advertising coordinator

Helen Murphy, former Director General, Information Management

Joanne Paré-Lacroix, secretarial support

Sheila Perron, secretarial support

Pierre Pontbriand, Director, Information Services

Claudette Roy, production coordinator

Colette Trudel, secretarial support.

INTRODUCTION

The Task Force on Sex-Role Stereotyping in the Broadcast Media had its beginnings in April 1979 when the former Minister of the Department of Communications, the Honourable Jeanne Sauvé, acting on an undertaking of the federal government in the National Plan of Action on the Status of Women,[10] wrote to the Chairman of the CRTC requesting that the Commission "take steps to see that guidelines and standards to encourage the elimination of sex-role stereotyping from the media it regulates are formulated."

"I am in favour," she stated, "of a task force with representatives drawn from the broadcasters, industry in general, advertisers, and women's groups." After receiving Madame Sauvé's request, the Commission initiated discussions with the advertising and broadcast industries to determine the most appropriate method for resolving the issue.

When Madame Sauvé's successor, the Honourable David MacDonald, assumed both the Communications portfolio and responsibility for the Status of Women, he reviewed the policy and budgetary implications and asked the Commission to continue its planning to establish a task force. The mandate remained the same. In an address entitled "Sex Stereotyping in the Media," presented to the Institute of Canadian Advertising, he said: "(The task force's) purpose will be to delineate guidelines for a more positive (and realistic) portrayal of women in radio and television (in both programming and commercials), and to make policy recommendations for consideration by the Commission and the broadcast industry. The task force could propose one of several mechanisms for the implementation of the guidelines it sets up: industry self-regulation, CRTC regulation, or government legislation. Which route will be the most effective will be up to the task force to decide."[11]

It was on 28 September 1979 that the CRTC formally announced the formation of the Task Force on Sex-Role Stereotyping to develop guidelines to encourage the elimination of sex-role stereotyping in the broadcast media. As detailed in the first pages of this report, under Composition of the Task Force, nineteen members were appointed. Included were four representatives from the advertising industry; four representing private broadcasting, and an appointee of the Canadian Broacasting Corporation; six representing the public interest; and four CRTC Commissioners. As well, two representatives from the Canadian Advisory Council on the Status of Women served as ex-officio members during their tenure as officers of the council.

In all, the Task Force held 12 meetings between 30 October 1979 and 29 March 1982. It scheduled six public meetings across Canada at which interested parties might present and discuss their views with a member of the Task Force. In addition, written submissions in the form of recommendations were solicited from the public.[12]

DEFINING THE PROBLEM

The Task Force on Sex-Role Stereotyping in the Broadcast Media, at its first meeting on 30 October 1979, agreed upon four points of reference. First, as the problem of sex-role stereotyping has already been well defined and well documented, the Task Force therefore would not undertake its own research.[13] Second, the Task Force considered the problem of sex-role stereotyping to be one of inequality and injustice rather than one of "bad taste." Third, the Task Force would give consideration to both commercials and programming, in that order; and finally, while recognizing that other forms of stereotyping can and do exist, it would concentrate on the sex-role stereotyping of women.

A. Sex-Role Stereotyping in the Broadcasting Environment

Stereotyped images of women and girls are reinforced and perpetuated, and to some extent even seemingly legitimized, by the mass dissemination of these images in broadcasting. Such images constitute a limiting or narrowing of women's, men's, and children's perceptions of themselves and their roles in society.

For those unfamiliar with the issues surrounding the problem of sex-role stereotyping, the following report may contain a number of relatively new ideas and observations. While these do not necessarily apply to every broadcast program or commercial, they do reflect a continuing public concern about sex-role stereotyping in the broadcast media.

Research into sex-role stereotyping has tended to focus on women rather than on men, television rather than radio, and on commercials more than on programming. But in study after study, the same conclusion is

3

reached, that the media do not portray women and men as equal, and equally capable, human beings. On this subject, the Nova Scotia Status of Women task force report stated: "(T)he image of women as portrayed not only in advertising but also in programming more often than not represents the damaging and inaccurate stereotype that is prevalent in our male-oriented society."[14]

B. The Representation of Women in the Broadcast Media

Women, like men, come in all ages, shapes, sizes, and colors, but are not so represented in the broadcast media. Nor is the increasing diversity of women's lives reflected in most broadcasting. For example, women are most often portrayed in programming and commercials as economically dependent homemakers, and mothers performing domestic tasks. This image predominates despite the fact that today most Canadian women, whether married or single, can expect to spend an average of 40 years in the labor force.[15]

When they are portrayed as members of the work force, women are shown in a much less representative range of occupations than men, and usually appear in stereotyped "female" areas of employment, such as secretarial or clerical work or nursing and teaching. Women rarely are presented in responsible decision making positions and few appear as blue collar workers. In many instances, women's careers are depicted as less important to them than romantic or family concerns.

Side by side with the stereotype of woman as homemaker and mother is the stereotype of woman as a sexual lure or decorative object. This aspect of women's portrayal is especially offensive to many. The fact that women are portrayed more often in this role than men, and through exaggerated acting, voice tone, and body language, serves to reinforce this stereotype.

4

Women in general, and women as homemakers in particular, are characterized as subservient to and/or dependent upon men. Men tell them what to do and their instructions seem to be gratefully accepted. In general, women are shown serving men and boys, but boys and men are rarely shown to serve women other than by opening doors or holding chairs, stereotypic evidence of women's apparent weakness or dependency. Women are often portrayed in isolation from each other or engaged in petty competition.

Most important, the image of woman in broadcasting is rarely that of an informed person or of a maker of decisions. In news and current affairs programming, women are seldom presented as experts; women's opinions are not sought as often as men's. Indeed women are invisible in the discussion of many issues. When dramatically portrayed, women usually are seen in less important roles and rarely are portrayed as informed and intelligent citizens. In commercial messages, women are seen as product users but not as principle product representatives or announcers. While women are portrayed as the potential or actual users of products, men are usually portayed as the "experts" and product demonstators.

Certainly, there are Canadian programs and commercials in which women are not subjected to stereotyped portrayals. At the same time, public concern has been expressed over the emergence of a new stereotype, the "superwoman" who can have a career and run a household without apparent effort, fatigue, or assistance from other family members.

C. The Cumulative Effect of Restricted Representation

It is not the isolated incident of portraying a woman in a stereotyped role that is at the center of public

5

criticism. When a program or commercial presents a stereotyped image of a woman or a man in a certain role, it may be acceptable for that particular role in that particular script. Rather, it is the cumulative effect of associating women and girls with certain roles, products, and behavior that is the source of concern. For example, when too many portrayals show the man as the breadwinner and the woman as the homemaker, the cumulative effect is that men and women become associated exclusively with those roles. An identical problem occurs when men and women appear again and again in traditional "male" or "female" jobs, perform only "male" or "female" tasks, and consistently display sex-stereotyped behavior.

The constant repetition of these images tends to reinforce their perceived reality, thus influencing the attitudes of women, men, and children, and encourages both women and girls to limit their horizons both socially and professionally to those roles which they see portrayed.[16]

D. Language

The use of language that excludes or patronizes women also serves to reinforce and sustain outmoded and inaccurate perceptions of women as a group. Repeated use of "he," "his," and words formed with "man" when referring to classes of work or groups of people effectively exclude women from their sense of place in a society where they are not just equal to men, but constitute 52 per cent of our population. For example, the words "businessmen and businesswomen" or "business people" would be more accurate than "businessmen" alone.

The continued use of demeaning and sexist language when referring to women is a related concern because of the negative imagery associated with it. Many women are offended or feel patronized when referred to as "chicks," "broads," "the weaker sex," "the little lady," and other such expressions, or in terms of their marital status or degree of physical appeal. Referring to adult females as "girls" is inaccurate, inappropriate, and demeaning.

Unequal treatment of the sexes through language is another source of concern. For example, referring to a married couple as "man and wife" labels the woman, but not the man, in terms of a role. "Man and woman" or "husband and wife" are more appropriate, and no less accurate, as descriptive expressions.

PUBLIC CONCERN

Canadian concern about sex-role stereotyping in broadcast programming and commercials has been evident for some time. Several submissions to the 1951 Royal Commission on National Development in the Arts, Letters and Sciences (the Massey Commission) discussed the portrayal of women. This concern was also expressed in the report of the 1970 Royal Commission on the Status of Women in Canada as well as in special reports by such diverse organizations as the Montreal YWCA,[17] the Nova Scotia Human Rights Commission,[18] and the Federation of Women Teachers' Association of Canada.[19] In addition, individual women and women's organizations have continued to make their objections known to broadcasters, to advertisers and their associated bodies, and to the CRTC.[20]

In 1979 the federal government published "Towards Equality for Women," the government's commitment to the women of Canada to equalize opportunities and ensure progress through a series of specific changes to government legislation, policies and programs. As a result of one of the commitments in that plan of action, the then Minister of Communications, the Honourable Jeanne Sauvé, requested that the CRTC establish this Task Force.

Concern about sex-role stereotyping also has been reflected in the growing body of Canadian research on this issue and in the increased responsiveness of the affected industries to the concerns expressed. For example, the advertising industry set up a task force of its own in 1976-77 that acknowledged the problem and provided guidelines for the creators and purchasers of advertising. This is significant even though such early recognition went largely unheeded, due in part to a lack of adequate promotion and to the fact that many in the industry were not prepared to concede the significance of the issue. Together, these activities highlight several years of increasing interest in, awareness of, and concern about sex-role stereotyping in broadcasting.

A. Call for Submissions

Because of differing perceptions and levels of awareness among its members, the Task Force decided to gauge for itself the intensity of public feelings about sex-role stereotyping. As mentioned in Chapter 1, the public was invited to submit its written comments and recommendations, and 124 submissions were received, ranging from simple one-paragraph letters to several major research briefs. The range of views was impressive. People from all walks of life took the time to write and to express their concern about this issue.

Six public meetings were scheduled by the Task Force to provide another forum for people to discuss their views on the subject. The meetings, held in February and March 1980, took place in Halifax, Montréal, Hull, Toronto, Edmonton, and Vancouver. At these public meetings, over 50 individuals, many representing large constituencies, urged the Task Force to find ways to eliminate sex-role stereotyping in programming and commercials.[21]

B. The Public Responds

There was one recurrent theme in both the submissions received by letter and those presented at the public meetings: that what is seen on television and heard on radio does not reflect adequately the realities of Canadian society.

> In contrast to the real changes that have occurred in our society, the broadcast media tend to perpetuate outmoded and unrealistic views of

9

women. Both in programming and in commercials,
women are most often portrayed as either
homemakers or sex objects. It is implied--both
explicitly and implicitly--that a woman's place is in
the home and that her only contribution to society
is the housework she performs. Alternatively
woman is exploited because of her sex; her primary
interest being depicted as that of "catching a
man," and once she has him, of serving and pleasing
him with little concern for her own worth or well-
being. The emphasis is placed on a woman's youth
and "decorative" features, instead of her
intelligence, ambitions or desires for her own self-
fulfillment.

> The Women's Bureau, Ontario
> Ministry of Labour

What follows is a sample of quotations reflecting some
of the major concerns and recommendations expressed
by members of the public in their briefs and letters to
the Task Force.[22]

> Certain categories of women, considered to be
> marginal, are scarcely represented: independent
> women, those from ethnic minorities or the
> working class, professionals and older women. The
> last-named appear only in the role of grandmothers
> touting the merits of products for the ill and the
> elderly (medication for arthritis, denture creams,
> laxatives, etc.). As a general rule, women in
> advertising live in luxury and comfort, and this
> portrayal of women is presented as being
> universally true (English translation).

> Annie Méar, Montréal[23]

Women, like men, come in all shapes, sizes and
ages. The media would have us believe that women
are acceptable only in one shape, size or age.

YWCA of Winnipeg

If today's advertisements were the only indication
of the modern woman's life-style it would appear
that we are all white, middle class, models,
housewives, and sexual objects. This is fully
supported not only by documentation, but by even
the skimpiest viewing of television or an hour's
worth of radio.

Feminist Party of Canada, Toronto

By far the largest number of television programs
considered "family entertainment," and the
commercials that punctuate them, present
outmoded, incorrect or prejudicial messages about
how men and women behave.

Women's Liaison Committee of the
Toronto Board of Education[24]

The model who walks her fingers through the
house, coping calmly with a thousand-and-one
chores while looking like a fashion mannequin is
also not true-to-life. She is more a male fantasy
than a female reality: the male concept of a
liberated woman.

Feminist Party of Canada, Toronto

Perhaps the most important feature of the treatment of women in television is the extent to which they are trivialized.

> Women Students' Office, University
> of British Columbia

Some pointed out the effects of such portrayals, first on children:

Girls are portrayed in much the same light as their mothers--little mothers, passive beauties who like nothing better than to play house and help with the chores in the kitchen. Such portrayals limit the aspirations and levels of achievement for most girls, and both sexes are influenced in their concepts of sex-roles, occupations, lifestyles, and other choices.

> The Women's Centre, Cranbrook,
> B.C.

--on all women:

(Advertising) legitimizes the idealized, stereotyped roles of women as temptress, wife, mother and sex-object and portrays women as less intelligent and more dependent than men. It makes women believe that their chief role is to please men and that their fulfillment will be as wives, mothers, and homemakers. ... It makes women believe that their own lives, talents and interests ought to be secondary to the needs of their husbands and families and that they are almost totally defined by these relationships.

> Women's Liaison Committee of the
> Toronto Board of Education

12

--on lesbians:

> The heterosexist bias of the media perpetuates discrimination against lesbians and gays and helps make our lives very dangerous and miserable; because those who rely on the media for their depiction of reality see us as sick or as non-existent and therefore as people to be hurt and destroyed.
>
> > Political Lesbians United about the Media, Toronto

Particular concern was voiced with regard to the language used in broadcast programming and commercials:

> Women should be referred to in parallel and equal status terms, not diminutive or demeaning terms.
>
> > P.E.I. Advisory Council on the Status of Women

> Parallel use of terms is another concern--if there is a men's team then the female counterpart should be called the women's team. Surely people would laugh uproariously if we talked of the gentlemen's hockey team or the boys' speed skating team (unless we truly meant juniors).
>
> > P.E.I. Advisory Council on the Status of Women

> The use of the word "man" and the attendant assumptions that it is the male figure that is the main actor gives a poor impression to young

13

women; it makes them feel ... makes us feel, as if
we have no past and no future. ... My
recommendation is that all broadcast media
seriously consider the words that they use, that the
word "man" when it refers not to males but to
human beings be completely eliminated in favor of
the words "human beings" or any one of a number
of words which portray the fact that human beings
come in two sexes.

Judith Wouk, Halifax

Some raised the issue of employment within
broadcasting:

Who has been able to watch a female athlete
without hearing incredulous exclamations
concerning her physical capabilities, of the sort,
"She's one heck of a little athlete!" ... or allusions
to her charm--or worse still, to her lack of charm?
Remember the female swimmers whose shoulder
muscles are particularly well-developed? When are
we going to see a female sports commentator?
(English translation).[25]

Réseau d'action et d'information pour
les femmes, Sillery, Québec

We would like to see women employed as
announcers on the national news on both networks
and also as foreign correspondents.

Port Coquitlam Area Women's
Centre, B.C.

I would like to see women have more input into our role in TV advertising--with an eye to portraying women in their proper role as educated, sophisticated individuals who are fed up with being portrayed as anything less.

Pauline Thompson, Swan Hills, Alta.

In programming, some noted that male perspectives predominate, and that attitudes toward women are often negative:

The fact that certain programs are represented as "women's" programs (through their title or scheduling) and that they are thus indicated to be intended for a female audience, seems at the same time to exclude women as viewers or participants in other programs which are directed toward the "general public" (social affairs, politics, the world of business or science, and so forth). In this way too, men are indirectly prevented from becoming interested in or improving their knowledge of activities which have traditionally been regarded as "women's" roles: cooking, handicrafts, plant care, and so forth. This categorization, which corresponds to the sex stereotyping of roles, must be avoided at all costs (English translation).

Réseau d'action et d'information pour les femmes, Sillery, Québec

Male perceptions of what is interesting, newsworthy and hence, good programming, are the rule.

YWCA of Winnipeg

There are television programs that I would like to mention: the first one ... started a couple of years ago. It started off with a picture of a male athlete and a male infant, and a fair amount of its content was in fact directed toward males. ... (I)n (some) context(s) there was no proof that it was a male that performed the action; for example, cave paintings ... were depicted as having been done by men, even though as far as I know there is no evidence to show that the sex of the painter is male.

Judith Wouk, Halifax

Women's contributions, issues, concerns, and activities receive less recognition than men's:

(E)vents which concern women still receive poor coverage: a ridiculously small amount of time is devoted to the event particularly if it occurs only once each year (March 8)[26]; and, contrary to the actual facts of the event, the involvement and interest of women is denied (English translation).

Réseau d'action et d'information pour les femmes, Sillery, Québec

Not enough program time is devoted to women. ...there is a lack of coverage on so-called women's issues, day care, employment problems, housing for the single parent, etc., on women in sports and women in their social, political and artistic contributions to society.

The Social Issues Committee, YWCA of Halifax

Programs which are likely to be of interest to
women are broadcast either at times which are
convenient only for women who are working in the
home or at times when the practical concerns of
the family prohibit close or meaningful attention
(English translation).

Réseau d'action et d'information pour
les femmes, Sillery, Québec

Just as women's role as child educator is ignored,
so too are the contributions of women to politics,
sciences, and the arts overlooked. As well as not
appearing frequently, women in credible roles are
under-represented; women as experts appear
infrequently. We believe women do contribute to
politics, sciences and the arts.

YWCA of Winnipeg

News coverage of feminist issues is treated as a
joke, made to look subversive, or shown in such a
fashion as to make the advocates look asinine. Too
often, the media distorts, humorizes, or disregards
the serious concerns of women. The feminist
movement has been sensationalized, demoralized,
misinterpreted, and ignored by the news media.
News coverage has lacked integrity and been
unethical in its presentation of women's issues.
Too often audio and visual clips are out of context
and the whole story is not told.

Women's Division, Saskatchewan
Labour

Many argued that, in advertising, women too often are exploited, treated as sex objects, put down, or insulted:

> Our suggestion for "Most Offensive Commercial" is the one in which Nonnie Griffiths points her chest at the audience and says, "My Harry thinks my full figure is a knockout!" It ends with "Harry" cupping his hand and grunting, "Eh?" This is a masterpiece of exploitation. How it ever received approval for broadcast is beyond our imagination. Words cannot describe the anger and resentment it inspires.
>
> North Bay Women's Centre

> Women are often portrayed as sex objects. They are shown to have a great need for personal adornment in order to attract and hold a man, and that would seem to be their whole "reason to be." What an insult to our intelligence!
>
> The Cranbrook Women's Resource Group, B.C.

> Commercials such as the "We're teasing Mrs. Baranowski about taking the whitener out of (a detergent)" is a devastating insult to women. Mrs. Baranowski apparently measures her entire value as a person by the condition of her child's T-shirts. And the cutsey approach suggests that the woman is so dim-witted that she can be tricked into taking the whole farce seriously. ... I view with concern the poor bewildered woman with clogged drains and the overpowering, god-like male voice telling the poor soul that she should use (a drain cleaner). What nonsense! I realize that advertising agencies must use gross exaggeration

18

and create dramatic effects to sell their products but I, for one, am turned off by that sort of thing.

Edith Torbay, Newsletter Editor of the North Bay Women's Centre

Many advertisements are not respectful of the part women play in the real world, usually ignoring their contributions completely, or so misrepresenting them that it becomes insulting at worst, or laughable, at best.

Patricia Newton, North Vancouver

A number of recent studies (L.J. Busby, 1975; J.D. Culley and R. Bennett, 1976; J.R. Dominick and G.E. Rauch, 1972; W.J. Lundstrom and D. Sciglimpaglia, 1977) seem to confirm what has long been apparent from daily observation, namely that the portrayal of women in advertising follows traditional stereotypes: mother, wife, house-keeper, and sex object--all of which roles advertising presents as reflecting reality. In the case of advertisements aimed specifically at men, women become decoration corresponding to the traditional canons of male desires (English translation).

Annie Méar, Montréal

Another complaint is about that toothpaste ... To refresh your memory--the man talks to his son as they stand back to back. He calls his wife and says angrily, "As long as I am paying his dental bill, he has to use such and such in his toothpaste!" The poor little mousey wife comes out of the kitchen and says, "Relax dear, he uses such and such!" I would not buy this toothpaste ever, because I resent men putting women down so much; and yet you keep allowing this kind of advertising to go on and on in TV and radio.

Juliette Gill, Victoria

Others noted the stereotyped, subservient manner in which women are portrayed, while their strengths and involvement in the labor force are minimized.

Relations between the members of couples as depicted in soap operas ... are almost always unbalanced, even unhealthy, with one member dominant and the other dominated, but are intended to represent the "normal" relations of the average couple. If the woman questions her role within the couple, or her identity, her most legitimate demands are quickly ridiculed on the pretext of interjecting a note of humor. Her crisis is resolved by the performance of the men and women around her, who point out that "she has no reason to be unhappy" and that, after all, her identity crisis was nothing more than a fit of hysteria, a momentary deviation for which she will try to earn forgiveness (English translation).

Réseau d'action et d'information pour les femmes, Sillery, Québec

I object most strongly to the TV advertisement for (a department store), which I saw on Sunday, 5 January 1980. The advertisement depicts a woman in an open car being approached by a motorcycle policeman. She is shown to be disorganized, cannot find her driver's licence in her

20

purse, bursts into tears, and passes the (facial tissue) to the cop. The policeman consoles her, tells her to relax and to go shopping at (a department store). My objection is directed to the not-so-subtle message that women (blonde) are disorganized, weepy, and can wheedle their way out of trouble with tears, which men (policemen) fall for, and excuse them of their responsibilities. The stereotype of weepy, dizzy blond women is totally abhorrent to today's women, who hold jobs, raise families, fix cars and are completely competent.

Jeanne Murphy and others, Victoria

A cold remedy commercial depicts the husband waking in the middle of the night with a miserable cold. He forces his wife to get up and take care of him. Wife is portrayed as a servant to man's needs; husband is portrayed as a weak character with no ability to look after himself.

Canadian Federation of University Women, Stratford

I feel obliged to write to complain about a particular advertisement I saw on Wednesday, November 21. It was aired during the "Raggedy Anne" Special. The commercial was for (a food product). ... It showed a very worn-out lady rushing home after a hard day and in a panic because her family expected supper shortly. (Food product) to the rescue!!! Meanwhile healthy looking dad and kids of approximate ages 7 and 10, also very healthy looking, are just sitting around the table. I didn't see a piano tied to their asses so why couldn't one of them help prepare the meal?...

21

It is very infuriating to see this kind of message
given to kids, especially during a program for kids,
that mother is a slave.

Linda Levesque, Regina

We strongly object that qualities such as display of
courage against odds, leadership in community and
national concerns, confidence in life roles,
intelligence and drive should be ascribed to one sex
alone.

Canadian Home Economics
Association, Toronto

For every woman in a commercial shown as a
professional, there are hundreds of standard
housewife roles. Little attention has been paid by
the advertising industry to the increasing number
of women joining the work force, and their
resulting impact on the economy as consumers with
ever-growing buying powers.

Feminist Party of Canada, Toronto

While the majority of those writing in response to the
Task Force's call for submissions were critical of the
way women are portrayed by the media, not all
respondents agreed with these criticisms:

We recommend that the first activity of the Task
Force be to find out whether there is a problem
before attempting to find the solution to it. It
should be recognized that advertising operates in
full public view and is dependent on its audience.
If advertising was displeasing to these audiences,
they would react against buying the products

22

advertised and either the products and companies concerned would die, or the advertising would change.

Canada Packers Ltd., Toronto

We submit that research has documented that sex-role stereotyping exists but it does not necessarily follow that it is a problem. Many research studies conducted by the advertising industry document that no serious problem exists. Indeed, rest assured that if a problem did exist the advertiser would quickly change his advertising since not to do so would prove detrimental to the sale of his product or service.

Canadian Imperial Bank of
Commerce, Toronto

Advertising often reflects society as it is rather than the way many would like society to be. It is unfair and unrealistic to expect advertisers to pay the costs of changing society's basic attitudes about life in general--though, as a company, we support the concept of equality of people generally.

The Quaker Oats Company of
Canada, Peterborough

I strongly oppose one more attempt by a government body to establish censorship on what the Canadian public can or cannot see, especially when that group can in no way be representative of the general public.

E.A. Roncarelli, Toronto

23

Many individuals and organizations, however, recommended that the advertising and broadcasting industries eliminate sex-role stereotyping and, instead, portray women in a respectful and realistic manner. Some suggestions were very specific:

> We want society to know that we are more than stereotypes, we want to show that both women and men can be strong, that both women and men can be nurturers, that no sex has the exclusive rights to logic or to intuition, to an interest in cleanliness or in foreign affairs. Men and women share human characteristics.
>
> Alberta Status of Women Action Committee and the YWCA of Calgary, Social Issues Committee

> We want to see women (and men) who are intelligent, strong, can relate to each other as genuine friends and equals, and are involved in a wide range of activities and occupations. They are of varied physical appearance, age, size, racial, and class background and style of dressing.
>
> Satellite Video Exchange Society, Vancouver

> What is presented as a liberated woman is often only a super sex object, with added male attributes or a traditionally male occupation. ... What is necessary are programs that truly reflect women's life experiences, values, and views of what liberation means.
>
> Women Students' Office, University of British Columbia

In order to encourage them to achieve their potential and to participate on an equal basis with men, women must be provided with realistic and unstereotyped role models so that attitudes towards various occupations and careers previously considered male domains can be changed.

> Canadian Federation of University
> Women, Head Office, Montréal

There should be equal male/female representation in all areas. The smarter, braver, more successful person should be a woman as often as a man.

> Women's Resource Centre,
> Peterborough Women's Committee

Men and women should be portrayed equally in the performance of all household and child-rearing tasks. They should appear interchangeably in sensitive and nurturing roles.

> Women's Liaison Committee of the
> Toronto Board of Education

We suggest ... that sexist advertising portraying the homemaker as an easily-influenced nonentity be eliminated and that where homemakers are portrayed, the managerial and decision making skills of this important role should be emphasized.

> Canadian Home Economics
> Association, Toronto

In recognition of already existing and documented changes in the division of labor within many families, men and children should be shown participating in a variety of household tasks.

> P.E.I. Advisory Council on the Status of Women

In programming for dramas, situation comedies, and documentaries, we would like to see a portrayal of the Canadian family as it is today, which includes single parents, couples without children, and widows and widowers.

> Port Coquitlam Area Women's Centre

Eliminate programming whose main thrust is the sex appeal of its characters.

> Canadian Federation of University Women, Stratford

Commercials could improve their impact if they showed people using products primarily to improve their sense of attractiveness to themselves. Most people choose brands because of greatest comfort or practicality--not because of someone else's needs.

> Canadian Federation of University Women, Stratford

The male as expert (as indicated by the high proportion of male voiceovers) must also be challenged. Women are experts and authorities in countless fields--they should be recognized as such.

P.E.I. Advisory Council on the Status of Women

The exclusive use of men as experts, even in fields that are stereotypically regarded as male, should be avoided.

British Columbia Teachers' Federation

Women must appear as effective persons and be shown by the broadcast media in positions of authority and competence as often as men.

National Council of Women of Canada, Ottawa

Members of women's associations should be consulted in the same way as business and labour organizations, on those events which concern them.

National Council of Women of Canada, Ottawa

Changes in the portrayal of women will occur only partially through the removal of existing sexist content. Positive change requires the extensive development of new content which is designed to portray women in the full range of their roles and experience, from their own perspective.

Joan Fraser, Halifax

27

As the above quotations show, a wide diversity of opinion was submitted to the Task Force by individuals from across Canada, all emphasizing their concern with the problem of sex-role stereotyping in the broadcasting media.

A SUMMARY OF CONCERNS

The following summary of concerns and possible solutions was compiled and discussed by the Task Force as a result of its examination of the literature, the written briefs, and its meetings with the public.

A. General Issues

i. Images

Although the word "image" tends to elicit thoughts of visual presentations, it also includes images evoked aurally. (This section therefore applies to both radio and television. The cumulative impact of stereotyped images is of special significance, and is applicable to many of the points made in this document.)

1. Broadcasting should include a wide variety of images reflecting the diversity of women in our culture. This includes:

    a. women of all ages (the elderly as well as the young);

    b. women of differing ethnic groups;

    c. women of differing physical appearance.

2. Broadcasting should present women engaged in a wide variety of activities, including athletics.

3. Women should not be used as sexual stimuli or lures, or as attention-getting, but otherwise irrelevant, objects.

4. Broadcasting should not demean or degrade women through the images used to portray them.

ii. Language

1. Language should be inclusive and non-sexist when all persons are meant to be included. The so-called "generic" man is inappropriate, as are diminutive terms such as "girl" or "little lady."

2. Broadcasting should not demean or degrade women through language, as it does when it refers to men in the context of their accomplishments and to women merely in terms of their appearance.

iii. Roles

1. Women should not be presented only in so-called traditional roles. The role of homemaker, for example, is but one of women's contemporary roles.

2. Women should be presented in a more balanced and realistic way in terms of their occupations or activities within contemporary society.

3. Men and children should be presented participating in household tasks.

4. Women are also authorities and experts and should be included and presented as such.

iv. Family and Interpersonal Relationships

1. When families are presented, the diversity of life styles that exist today should be reflected (for example, single parents and extended families).

2. Women should not be presented as subservient to and dependent on men.

3. Men should not be presented as always being the beneficiaries of services performed by women or products used by women.

4. No interpersonal relationship or lifestyle that is consistent with the maintenance of human dignity should be demeaned or degraded in broadcasting.

v. Personality

1. Motives and needs

   a. Broadcasting should not play on women's fears, such as the fear of being sexually unattractive.

   b. Women should not be presented as either excessively concerned with youth and beauty or neurotically afraid of aging.

   c. Women should not be presented as being neurotically compulsive about cleanliness.

   d. Broadcasting should not imply that the prime motivating factor for a woman is to catch a man.

2. Traits

   a. Broadcasting should not demean or degrade women by presenting them as possessing predominantly negative traits, for example, "catty," "bitchy," dependent, incompetent, subservient, submissive, and so forth.

3. Intellectual Factors

   a. Broadcasting should not involve a condescending presentation of women's intelligence and capabilities. It is demeaning

and degrading to portray women as
unintelligent and incapable.

   b. Women should be presented as decision makers,
       and contributing significantly to society.

B. Programming

In addition to all of the concerns in the above section,
the following apply specifically to programming.

i. News, Public Affairs, Documentaries, Arts and/or
Sciences

1. Women should be more adequately represented as
    news readers, reporters, and hosts.

2. Issues of special concern to women, such as sexual
    harrassment, rape, or equal pay legislation, should
    receive more adequate coverage.

3. Women's events (such as conferences,
    demonstrations, press releases) should receive
    attention and coverage equal to that given to men's
    events.

4. Women's contributions (for example in the artistic,
    scientific, economic fields) should be recognized
    and presented fairly.

5. Women's perspectives on issues of general interest
    (for example, the economy, elections, international
    events) should be included adequately in general
    reporting and comment (women as experts or
    authorities, and/or in giving public views).

ii. Sports

1. Participation of women in sports should receive
    fair and equitable coverage.

2. Women athletes should not be subject to patronizing or belittling treatment.

iii. Drama, Variety, Humor, Children's Programming

1. Many of these concerns are discussed in the first section, General Issues.

2. A balance of female and male perspectives should be represented in stories, issues, topics, and images, as well as in writing, editing, directing, and producing.

C. Radio

In addition to all of the concerns in the first two sections, the following apply specifically to radio:

1. Those who select music for broadcasting purposes should be sensitive to the often violent, sexist, and racist lyrics of some popular music, and should not use such offensive material.

2. Music by women artists and composers should be better represented in the selection of listening material offered to the public.

3. Broadcasters should be sensitive to their use of language and images to avoid sexist and demeaning treatment of women. This is important especially for hot line hosts and radio personalities.

4. Women should be adequately represented as D.J.s and program hosts, in particular as hot line hosts.

D. Commercials

In addition to the concerns expressed in the first section, the following apply specifically to commercials:

i. Women as Buyers

1. Women should not be presented in desperate need either of products or of assumed product benefits in order to meet alleged deficiencies or in order to satisfy or serve their adult companions or children.

2. Women buy a full range of products and services (including, for example, cars and bank loans), and commercials should reflect this more fairly.

3. Women are not the exclusive buyers and users of products for the home, and commercials should reflect this as well.

4. Products such as cosmetics, fragrances, jewellery, and clothing should be presented as personally beneficial, not as a means to catch or please a man.

ii. Women as Sellers

1. Women should be presented as experts and authorities as well as men.

2. Voice-overs on TV and announcers on radio should be female as well as male (they are predominantly male now).

3. Women should be shown selling a wider range of products and services, not only those assumed to be for women.

E. Other

1. Feminine hygiene advertising is particularly offensive to many people and therefore needs to be dealt with by advertisers in a sensitive and informative manner.[27]

2.   Male dominance and female submissiveness are at the very heart of the stereotypes of men and women. Pornography reflects the extreme portrayal of dominance and the exploitation of women's sexuality. Pornography, or any portrayal of violence against women, is the ultimate expression of dominance/submissiveness, the objectification of women. As such, pornography or the portrayal of violence against women has no place in the broadcast media.

EXISTING GOVERNMENT REGULATION AND INDUSTRY SELF-REGULATION

A. Government Regulation

i. The Role of the CRTC

Regulation of broadcasting in Canada is the responsibility of the CRTC. All broadcasting undertakings are operated under a licence issued by the Commission for a period not exceeding five years, following a public hearing to which the public is invited to submit interventions. Interventions are also invited for applications for renewal and amendment of licences, which also may result in a public hearing. The Broadcasting Act grants the CRTC jurisdiction over broadcast programming and commercials on both radio and television. However, there are no federal regulations that address sex-role stereotyping in either broadcast programming or commercials.

ii. Government of Québec Advertising Guidelines

One provincial government, the Government of Québec, established voluntary advertising guidelines in December 1979 specifically designed to reduce the incidence of sex-role stereotyping in all types of advertising.[28] Responsibility for providing information about the guidelines belongs to le Comité pour la publicité non-sexiste, a sub-committee of le Conseil du statut de la femme (the Québec advisory council on the status of women).

B. Industry Self-Regulation

Various organizational structures have been established within the broadcasting and advertising industries for the purpose of setting self-regulatory guidelines, policies, or codes of standards, with respect to both program and commercial content. This section will describe briefly existing self-regulatory organizations and mechanisms in both industries, and review those self-regulatory activities that address the issue of sex-role stereotyping.

i. Programming

In the public sector, the Canadian Broadcasting Corporation regulates the content of CBC programming through its policies. It now has two program policies and guidelines that specifically address the representation of women in all its programming: a policy on the portrayal of women in programming, a policy on stereotypes in CBC programs, and a set of language guidelines, in both English and French.[29]

In the private sector, individual station licensees are responsible for programs that are broadcast. All stations are responsible for their programming content. The Canadian Association of Broadcasters (CAB) is a voluntary association of privately-owned radio and television stations and networks. Member stations of the CAB adhere to the voluntary code of ethics of the CAB,[30] which serves to guide station licensees and managers in the formulation of their policies regarding program content.

The Broadcasters' Code of Ethics was developed by the CAB for voluntary use by proprietors and managers of member broadcasting services. The code addresses many aspects of broadcasting, in addition to programming and commercials in general. While it currently contains no specific references to the presentation of the sexes, the CAB is now reviewing recommendations for change.

ii. Commercials

In the case of broadcasting commercials, all broadcast entities require that commercials conform to their particular commercial acceptance policies. In general, commercial acceptance requires that the material meet standards of "good taste." Standards may vary according to individual corporate policies.

In the case of the CBC, it has gone further and added an anti-discrimination clause. It reads, in part, as follows:

> Commercials that have the effect of demanding audience attention by the use of shock value and double entendre, or that exploit sex or nudity to achieve this purpose go against the normal standards of good taste.

and:

> ...individuals or groups must not because of age, occupation, creed, or sex be disparaged or unfairly represented. The Corporation is sensitive to sex-role stereotyping in broadcast advertising, and believes advertisers should endeavor to represent both sexes fairly in all types of roles.[31]

In the case of the advertising industry, self-regulation occurs through the Advertising Advisory Board (AAB)[32] and the Advertising Standards Council (ASC) for English-speaking communities across Canada; and la Confédération générale de la publicité (COGEP) and le Conseil des normes de la publicité, for French-speaking communities. These non-profit organizations are funded by advertisers, advertising agencies, and media. The AAB and COGEP are responsible for public information, research, and education on advertising. The ASC and le Conseil des normes, which include public representatives, are autonomous, independent bodies responsible for administering industry self-regulatory codes of standards.

The Canadian Code of Advertising Standards is one of the codes administered by the ASC and le Conseil des normes de la publicité, and is the general self-regulatory code for all advertising. Prior to its amendment in 1980, this code dealt primarily with various aspects of misleading advertising. Complaints concerning the portrayal of individuals and groups were regarded by the councils as matters of "taste and opinion," outside the purview of the code.

On 1 July 1980, the code was amended to include a clause that covers taste, opinion, and public decency. Clause 15 states in part: "advertising shall not present demeaning or derogatory portrayals of individuals or groups and should not contain anything likely, in the light of generally prevailing standards, to cause deep or widespread offence."[33]

Although this clause does not specifically refer to sex-role stereotyping, complaints about commercials that are obvious violations of Clause 15 can be referred to the councils for action. Should the councils find that a commercial violates the code, and should the advertiser refuse to amend or withdraw the message, media are notified of the contravention and the commercial ceases to appear. The Canadian Association of Broadcasters has endorsed the Canadian Code of Advertising Standards, and the CBC has endorsed it in principle.

iii. Employment

Usually, any corporate organization wishing to ensure equal employment opportunities for potential employees, and advancement opportunities for individuals already on staff, will first adopt an equal opportunity policy and then, if it is deemed necessary to correct the existing imbalance, will also adopt an affirmative action program (or policy). Whereas equal opportunity is a permanent policy to ensure non-discrimination in hiring and promotion practices, affirmative action is a temporary measure adopted to seek out members of under-represented groups through hiring and promotion programs designed to increase their numbers.

The CBC has established a permanent equal opportunity policy[34] as well as a temporary affirmative action program for women that is designed to ensure that the equal opportunity policy has tangible results.

The CTV network is considering publishing its employment policy regarding equal opportunity and promotion on merit.

INDUSTRY CONCERNS AND RESPONSES

During the course of the Task Force discussions, both broadcasters and advertisers raised a number of concerns regarding the potential impact of possible regulatory action and of Task Force involvement with respect to stereotyping. This chapter, in addition to detailing industry responses to the problem at hand, also summarizes these concerns.

A. Concerns

i. The Question of Creativity

Broadcasters and advertisers both expressed to the Task Force their concern that regulation, or the institution of guidelines with respect to sex-role stereotyping, could interfere with their creative freedom, thus limiting both industries in their commercial endeavors. Advertisers noted that, in order to communicate their message effectively in a 30- or 60-second time frame, they must employ a variety of creative techniques that are appropriate both to the product itself and to the audience they are trying to reach.

Creative freedom is of paramount importance to broadcasters in the production of programs designed to appeal to a large number of viewers or listeners. For this reason, the CAB's Special Committee on Sex-Role Stereotyping noted that broadcasters "are therefore always concerned about influences ... which may be brought to bear upon those aspects of creativity and spontaneity in such a way as to limit or minimize their effective and valued contributions to programming."[35]

However, some members of the Task Force suggested that creative freedom is never absolute within a commercial context because creators of broadcast programs and commercials are always required to work

41

within constraints of time, budget, and theme or message. Indeed, some suggested that, rather than inhibiting the creative process, a non-stereotypic approach might even stimulate creativity by encouraging the production of innovative material.[36]

ii. The Private Broadcasting Industry

Private broadcasters brought a number of concerns before the Task Force. First and foremost, broadcasters expressed a concern that the Task Force take into account the economic realities of broadcasting in the formulation of its recommendations. Within the private broadcasting industry, all programming decisions are made in direct response to the market place. Scheduling decisions, for example, are determined by audience size for a particular program; foreign programs are selected on the basis of their proven popularity. In order to realize competitive advantage, broadcasters explained, flexibility in making such decisions is essential. New regulations likely would have a limiting effect on this flexibility.

Broadcasters stated that they were becoming more sensitive to the issue at hand; and, in recognizing the validity of the concerns expressed, are committed to reflecting in programming the changing role of women in society. When considering guidelines, broadcasters stressed that it should be recognized that great change is not likely to be accomplished overnight; nor is it likely that stereotyping, whatever its focus, will completely disappear from broadcast programming.

iii. The Advertising Industry

Members of the advertising community raised a number of specific concerns during the course of the Task Force's deliberations. At the outset, advertisers expressed their concern that the public perceived advertising as having more responsibility in the overall problem of sex-role stereotyping than was actually warranted. Advertisers agreed that a problem existed and admitted having contributed to it. At the same time, they stressed that they had not created the problem of sex-role stereotyping; they also noted that it is not within the power of advertisers alone to correct the problem.

In this context, advertisers requested that the Task Force acknowledge the legitimate role of advertising in the economy and its value to the broadcast industry in particular; and they expressed their concern that the commercial realities of the advertising business, and its attendant constraints, be taken into consideration in determining solutions. Advertisers stressed the fact that stereotyping is a legitimate advertising technique, of which negative stereotyping is only a small part. Consumer response to commercials is very diverse, and it is difficult for an advertiser working within a 30-second time frame to decide to which reaction to respond in order to sell a product. The reality of a fragmented market requires a variety of commercials to address broadcasting's diverse audience. Stereotyping is one method available to advertising agencies attempting to reach a wider audience.

Finally, the advertising community urged the Task Force to recognize the opportunity that existed for self-regulation by the industry. They stated that whatever recommendations finally were made, it was not realistic to expect immediate change in all advertising activity; and that increased awareness of, and sensitivity to, the problem on the part of the advertising community were more realistic short-term goals.

B. Responses

i. The Canadian Broadcasting Corporation

Public concern regarding the portrayal of women in CBC programming and commercials was brought formally to the attention of the CBC first during the hearing of its 1974 licence renewal application. In the introduction to their joint brief to the CRTC, Women for Political Action and the Ontario Committee on the Status of Women explained that their purpose in intervening was to seek the elimination of the time lag between the presentation of women in most CBC television programming and commercials, and the reality of most women's lives. It was pointed out that, while in 1974 women represented over one-half of the population and more than 30 per cent of the labor force, they were significantly under-represented in CBC programming and, when present in programming and commercials, tended to be portrayed in traditional, sex-stereotyped roles. A further concern was that, overall, the image of women projected on CBC television was degrading and sexist.[37]

The same brief also raised the issue of equality of opportunity for women employees of the CBC. It was noted therein that, although evidence indicated that women employees did not receive equal treatment within the Corporation, no commitment had been made by senior management to rectify this situation. The intervenors admonished the CBC for failing to implement the recommendations made to federal Crown corporations and agencies by the Royal Commission on the Status of Women, and urged their immediate adoption.

Concern regarding the portrayal of women in CBC broadcast programming and commercials was also brought to the attention of the Corporation's 1974 Task

44

Force on the Status of Women in the CBC. Although these matters, strictly speaking, were outside the mandate of that task force, its members nonetheless recommended that the CBC examine the issue of the portrayal of women in programming, and establish "more clear-cut commercial acceptance guidelines."

Programming

The public's growing concern over the portrayal of women in CBC programming was demonstrated during the CBC's 1978 licence renewal hearing before the CRTC, when six women's organizations submitted briefs calling on the CBC to address this problem.[38] These briefs reiterated and expanded upon the points made during the 1974 hearing, and noted that several of these concerns had not yet been addressed. Several pointed out that, as a public entity, the CBC had a special responsibility to reflect in its programming the reality of Canadian women's lives. Responding to these interventions, the President of the CBC, A.W. Johnson, undertook before the CRTC to invite representatives of major women's organizations to attend a seminar during which he proposed to hold discussions on programming issues. The seminar, held at the CBC Head Office on 22-23 February 1979, was attended by representatives of each of the six women's organizations, as well as by representatives of the Canadian Advisory Council on the Status of Women and the National Council of Women in Canada. Recommendations were made and discussed, and at the conclusion of the seminar, the CBC made a number of commitments to improve the Corporation's program and commercial content. A summary of these commitments,[39] and action taken to date, follows:

- To develop a program policy on the portrayal of women in CBC programming.

This program policy has been in effect since 10 December 1979. A policy on stereotypes in CBC programming has been in effect since 27 June 1980.

- To develop guidelines to eliminate sexist bias and language.

Guidelines have been developed in French and English to encourage the use of inclusive language and to discourage the use of sexist language. These were distributed to all CBC staff in Spring 1980.

- To establish a process of program evaluation to monitor implementation of objectives.

In 1981, the CBC commissioned two major independent research studies[40] that describe, by means of a content analysis, the portrayal of women and men in prime time on the English and French television networks of the CBC. Subsequent phases of this research will describe how these portrayals are perceived by the general public, women's organizations, and CBC production personnel.

Public members of the Task Force expressed concern that this independent research would not be comparable to previous monitoring studies done by the Corporation in 1979 and 1980, and requested that the Corporation undertake, on a regular basis, studies of a comparative nature that would make it possible to evaluate progress. The CBC has committed itself to monitor news and current affairs programming again in 1982.[41]

- To create two positions for social affairs specialists in TV news, one each in the English and French networks, to ensure comprehensive coverage of issues of concern to women.

These two positions at the Montréal and Toronto news desks were filled in August 1979 and June 1980 respectively.

- To develop awareness sessions on sex-role stereotyping and sexist imagery for CBC production staff.

Twelve sensitization seminars were held for management staff of the CBC English Services Division in Winter 1980. Because an evaluation of the sessions revealed that they had not met expectations, a new series is being developed for presentation in both French and English.

To coordinate the implementation of these commitments, and to receive and process complaints, the position of Coordinator, Portrayal of Women in Programming, was created in May 1979 within the Corporation's Corporate Affairs Division.

- To host a follow-up meeting with representatives of women's organizations to assess the effectiveness of the initiatives undertaken.

This commitment was met in June 1980. While no subsequent formal meetings have taken place between management and women's groups, the Coordinator, Portrayal of Women in Programming, has participated in a number of public workshops and given lectures on sex stereotyping in broadcast programming to various women's groups.

However, when the Task Force discussed the CBC proposal, the three public members who attended the CBC seminar pointed out to the Corporation's representatives that several of what they considered to be key commitments had not been acted on in a manner that was satisfactory to them. In particular, these were:

47

1. the commitment by management to hold periodic consultations with women's groups;

2. the commitment to a regular evaluation, by unit heads, of progress within their departments towards implementation of Corporation policies and guidelines on sex-role stereotyping.

Employment

On the issue of employment, the Corporation's formal response to the concerns expressed within the CBC by its women employees, and before the CRTC, was the formation in May 1974 of the Corporation's Task Force on the Status of Women in the CBC. (Mention of this task force is first made in the introduction to this section.) The mandate of the task force was to examine the status of the CBC's women employees, and to develop programs and accompanying organizational mechanisms to improve women's employment opportunities within the Corporation.

On the basis of its study, the CBC task force concluded that women employees of the CBC did have legitimate cause for concern, particularly in the area of job access. Altogether, some 50 recommendations were made to CBC management under the categories of occupational representation, advancement, training, compensation, employment, treatment on the job, and responsibilities of parenthood. While, strictly speaking, the status of women on contract lay outside the mandate of the CBC task force, concern was such that additional recommendations were made in this area.[42] Most of the CBC task force recommendations were accepted by CBC management and, to date, 34 of them either have been implemented, or are in the process of being implemented, with seven more on going.[43]

The Corporation agreed to undertake a long-term equal opportunity program, and an Office of Equal Opportunity was established to oversee its implementation. Since the office opened in 1975, the CBC has developed and circulated an Equal Opportunity Policy; held attitude awareness seminars and briefings for managers; and arranged career awareness seminars for women employees. The office also monitors progress made under its various programs on an ongoing basis.

As a result of these initiatives, the CBC feels that significant progress has been made both in eliminating systemic discrimination in hiring and promotion practices, and in the movement of women into management, program production, and journalism.[44] The most recent initiative resulting from this program is the adoption in principle by the CBC Board of Directors of the Office of Equal Opportunity's recommendation to establish an affirmative action program for the Corporation's women employees.

Broadcast Commercials

The CBC responded in part to public concern regarding the portrayal of women in commercials broadcast by the network when it committed itself during the 1979 CBC seminar to conducting a review of its commercial content. This was done by means of an internal study that was completed in Winter 1980. Commercials taped for that study since have been used to sensitize CBC staff to sex-role stereotyping in broadcast commercials. To date, three formal sessions plus a number of workshops have taken place, and more of both are planned for the future. The CBC also committed itself to participating in a dialogue with the CRTC and other broadcasters on this issue. This commitment was furthered when the CBC agreed to sit as a member of the Task Force on Sex-Role Stereotyping in the Broadcast Media.[45]

Within this forum, public members reiterated the recommendation that the CBC establish commercial acceptance standards for the portrayal of women in broadcast commercials. Specifically, public members recommended that the CBC amend its Commercial Acceptance Code "to include a new section on inclusive language, non-derogatory portrayal of women and proportionate representation in all ads, where appropriate." In June 1980, the CBC responded in part to these concerns by amending its Commercial Acceptance Policy Directive on standards of good taste in commercial presentation to include the following statement on sex-role stereotyping. This statement reads:

> Also individuals or groups must not because of age, occupation, creed or sex be disparaged or unfairly represented. The Corporation is sensitive to sex-role stereotyping in broadcast advertising, and believes advertisers should endeavor to represent both sexes fairly in all types of roles.[46]

The CBC has accepted, in principle, the advertising guidelines released by this Task Force in November 1980, and a representative of the Corporation sits as an observer on the AAB Advisory Committee on Sex-Role Stereotyping. The Corporation has purchased copies of "Women Say the Darndest Things," a film commissioned by the AAB for the purpose of promoting understanding of the task force advertising guidelines. This film has been distributed to all regional offices.

ii. Educational Broadcasters

Five provincially-funded educational broadcasting entities are active in Canada. The Knowledge Network in British Columbia, Radio-Québec, the Ontario Educational Communications Authority (OECA), and the Alberta Educational Communications Corporation

(ACCESS Alberta) all originate programming; while the Saskatchewan Educational Communications Corporation (SASKMEDIA) acquires and produces educational programming for provincial distribution. While these organizations were not represented formally on the Task Force, when they were contacted by it, all expressed interest in the project.

In addition, OECA made available to the Task Force an internal study that it had undertaken, which examined male and female roles in both production and acting positions in its programming. The study, "Male and Female Roles in OECA Programming," was published in 1976,[47] and Maxene Raices, the study's project officer, attended a task force meeting to discuss the results and methodology.

iii. The Private Broadcasting Industry

Actions taken by the private broadcasting industry in response to public concern over sex-role stereotyping in broadcast programming were stimulated by the participation of CAB representatives on this Task Force. The first step taken toward developing a proposal to the Task Force came in April 1981, when the CAB passed a resolution on sex-role stereotyping at its annual general meeting. The resolution acknowledged that sex-role stereotyping was a problem and a committee was established to formulate recommendations on how radio and television members of the Association could, through self-regulation, improve the image of women in broadcast programming.

The Special Committee of the CAB presented its "Sex-Role Stereotyping Report" to the Task Force in September 1981.[48] Contained therein were five recommendations, as follows:

1. That the CAB Code of Ethics be amended, first, to include a new clause on human rights, making it the responsibility of broadcasters to ensure, to the best of their ability, that their programming contains no abusive or discriminatory material or comment relating to either sex. This clause will read:

> Recognizing that every person has a right to full and equal recognition and to enjoy certain fundamental rights and freedoms, broadcasters should endeavor to ensure, to the best of their ability, that their programming contains no abusive or discriminatory material or comment which is based on matters of race, national or ethnic origin, color, religion, age, sex, marital status, or physical or mental handicap.

The CAB Code of Ethics also will call upon members to incorporate CAB endorsement and support for the guidelines of the advertising industry in dealing with the issue of sex-role stereotyping. The code will include a new clause addressing the issue of sex-role stereotyping that will read:

> Recognizing that stereotypic images can and do cause negative and countervailing influences, it shall be the responsibility of the broadcasters to reflect, to the best of their ability, a conscious sensitivity to the problems related to sex-role stereotyping by refraining from exploitation and by reflection of the intellectual and emotional equality of both sexes in programming.

2. That the CAB develop its own program for sensitizing its members to the issue of sex-role stereotyping as it relates to program production.

3. That the CAB immediately embark on a public information program to identify the Association's concern and actions with regard to this issue.

4. That the CAB support the voluntary initiatives of the advertising industry and extend, wherever possible, its cooperation.

5. That the CAB exercise its best efforts to incorporate inclusive language in production, avoiding wherever possible expressions that relate to one gender.

In responding to the special committee report, public members of the Task Force made a number of suggestions to the CAB to improve and further refine their voluntary initiatives. First, public members expressed their opinion that, in order for the CAB proposal for self-regulation to be as effective as possible, a mechanism for the handling and processing of complaints from the public should be established. CAB agreed that the Special Committee on Sex-Role Stereotyping would be reconstituted for this purpose. Secondly, public members asked CAB to provide some added details on the educational program proposed in the special committee report and offered their assistance in the development of this program. It was also agreed that a list of specific programming concerns about sex-role stereotyping would be distributed to CAB members.

In October 1981, the CAB Board of Directors received and accepted the report and recommendations of the special committee and, in addition, passed the following resolutions:

- That a workshop on sex-role stereotyping be held at the next CAB annual meeting.

- That the CAB implement recommendations 2 and 3 of its "Sex-Role Stereotyping Report" by developing and implementing most of its program as soon as possible, early in 1982.

- That, as part of its program, the CAB examine the possibility of producing master tapes concerning the topic of sex-role stereotyping and to use its program exchange service for the dissemination of this material.

- That the CAB revive its Committee on Sex-Role Stereotyping to serve as the responsible body to examine complaints received from the public, and to advise on the implementation of all CAB recommendations on sex-role stereotyping. Either this committee or the CAB Education Committee will be responsible for the educative role proposed in the report.

The general membership of the CAB will be asked to approve the resolutions of the board at its next general meeting, set for Fall 1982.

iv. The Advertising Industry

The Canadian advertising industry previously had addressed the issue of sex-role stereotyping and the portrayal of women in advertising in 1976, with the establishment of its Task Force on Women and Advertising.[49] The industry task force published a report in November 1977 entitled, "Women and Advertising, Today's Messages--Yesterday's Images?"[50]

In setting out its conclusions, this report acknowledged that sex stereotyping in advertising was indeed a problem. In its recommendations, therefore, the report urged advertisers and advertising agencies to re-evaluate their advertising and attempt to portray women in a more positive and realistic manner. No recommendations were made for institutional or regulatory change within the industry.

Subsequently, the advertising industry has recognized that one of the problems with the report was the lack of funds to distribute its findings, conclusions, and suggestions. A more widely publicized forum for debate on specific issues of concern was provided by the establishment in 1979 of the present Task Force on Sex-Role Stereotyping in the Broadcast Media. Within this forum, public members of the Task Force argued the case for amending the Canadian Code of Advertising Standards to include offensive portrayal of women as a ground for complaint to the Advertising Standards Council and le Conseil des normes de la publicité.[51]

The Advertising Standards Council and le Conseil des normes de la publicité already had held discussions on amending the code in response to such concerns. The July 1980 revision of the code included a clause responding to some of the concerns raised. Clause 15, "Taste, Opinion and Public Decency," already mentioned in Chapter 5, "Government Regulation and Industry Self-Regulation," in the treatment of advertising industry self-regulation, reads as follows:

> a. As a public communications process, advertising should not present demeaning or derogatory portrayals of individuals or groups and should not contain anything likely, in the light of generally prevailing standards, to cause deep or widespread offense. It is recognized, of course, that standards of taste are subjective and vary widely from person to person and community to community, and are, indeed, subject to constant change.
>
> b. The authority of the Code and the jurisdiction of the Council are over the content of advertisements. The Code is not meant to impede in any way the sale of products which some people, for one reason or another, may find offensive--provided, of course,

that the advertisements for such products do not contravene section a. of this Clause.

Public members of the Task Force felt that these changes did not go far enough. At the outset, advertising industry members of the Task Force stated that they preferred to deal with the concerns raised regarding sex-role stereotyping in advertising by developing a set of positive action statements for voluntary use by their members, instead of regulation. It was agreed that the advertising industry would be given an opportunity to develop a proposal for self-regulation. Public members expressed their willingness to provide assistance, and did in fact participate in the development of such a proposal. As a first step, advertising industry representatives requested and received an organized summary of the public members' concerns and recommendations pertaining to sex stereotyping in commercials. On 31 July 1980, industry representatives presented their formal brief to the Task Force.[52]

The brief contained nine positive action statements developed and endorsed by the industry for use by its members.[53] To promote awareness of these statements, the industry also committed itself to an implementation plan that reflected the main concerns brought forward during the Task Force meetings. The plan consisted of the establishment of a mechanism, in the form of advisory committees, for the receipt and processing of complaints about sex-role stereotyping in advertising; for the development of a sensitization program for industry members that would include the production of an audio-visual presentation; and for an on going research program to determine benchmarks for the future evaluation of the entire program. These initiatives were to be funded by the advertising industry. The proposed program for self-regulation would be implemented in French-speaking communities throughout Canada by la Confédération générale de la publicité (COGEP).

In their written response to the industry's brief, public members accepted the proposed guidelines with specific wording changes to the guidelines both on language and on voiceovers, experts, and authorities. Recommendations also were made and accepted for the membership and terms of reference of the proposed advisory committees, and for the implementation of the proposed guidelines. The final version of the advertising industry proposal was adopted by the Task Force and immediately released to the public to facilitate early implementation.

The AAB advisory committee on sex-role stereotyping, which receives and processes complaints from English-speaking communities across Canada, is comprised of advertising agency members, advertisers, broadcasters, members of the print media, and public representatives, including representatives of recognized feminist organizations and of the Consumers Association of Canada. The committee's existence has been widely publicized. Fifteen thousand copies of a brochure explaining objectives have been mailed to advertisers, advertising agencies and associations, media management people, and to many organizations and individuals outside the industry. Agencies also have been encouraged to use the committee as a consultative body for advertising. Committee members have addressed a number of industry and public groups on the subject of the committee mandate and the advertising guidelines. The film, "Women Say The Darndest Things," commissioned by the AAB to promote understanding of the guidelines, has been screened during these gatherings and made available on request to interested advertisers, advertising agencies, media, trade associations, and other parties.

The COGEP advisory committee receives and processes complaints from French-speaking communities across Canada. Le Comité pour la publicité non-sexiste, established by the Status of Women Council to administer the Government of Québec anti-discrimination guidelines, has now agreed to forwarding complaints it receives on sex-role stereotyping in advertising to the COGEP committee for processing.

Preparatory work for the development of a national attitude study on advertising, which also examines public attitudes toward sex-role stereotyping, is being undertaken during 1982 by the AAB and COGEP.

TASK FORCE ACHIEVEMENTS AND RECOMMENDATIONS

A. The Broadcasting Environment

Whether publicly or privately owned, the various participating organizations in the Canadian broadcasting environment operate in a competitive market. In the case of the private sector, all of its revenue is derived from the sale of commercial time. The Task Force recognizes that Canadian broadcasting is an evolving creative process, often operating in competition with foreign signals and commercials; and it is against this background that recommendations for the improved portrayal of women in the broadcast media were made.

i. Imported and Foreign Signals

Most Canadians have access to programs and commercials that originate from broadcasting sources in the United States. Any guidelines and regulations put into effect in Canada could not be applied to the over-the-air reception of broadcast signals that originate in foreign countries.

B. Task Force Achievements

This section contains a summary of measures dealing with sex-role stereotyping in Canadian broadcasting, which were developed during the course of the Task Force deliberations and are already in place.

i. The Canadian Broadcasting Corporation

The existence of the Task Force, and the CBC's representation on it, has acted as an incentive for the Corporation, first, to follow up on certain of its previously made commitments regarding the portrayal of women in programming and commercials;[54] and second, to undertake new activities, in parallel with the work of the Task Force.

In May 1979, the Corporation appointed a full-time coordinator responsible for the implementation of the Corporation's public commitments.[55] The Coordinator, Portrayal of Women in Programming, also sat as the CBC representative on the Task Force. While the Corporation already had made a public commitment to evaluate its progress in the portrayal of women in programming, criticism had been expressed internally concerning the validity of monitoring efforts undertaken in 1979 and 1980. In order to dispel any doubts as to the validity of these monitoring efforts, and to establish a firm basis for future comparisons, the Corporation recently undertook two major content analysis studies.[56] These are intended to be used for awareness seminars and information sessions, and they will also form the basis for future monitoring studies of sex-role stereotyping in CBC television programming. Furthermore, the Corporation agrees with the public members' request that the results of these studies be made public. Clarification of the CBC Commercial Acceptance Code with respect to the portrayal of women in broadcast commercials was also, in part, a result of debate on this issue within the Task Force.[57] The CBC has accepted in principle the Task Force guidelines on advertising.

ii. The Private Broadcasting Industry

Stimulated by its participation on the Task Force, the CAB has undertaken the following measures:[58]

1. The Association's Executive will recommend to the 1982 general meeting that the CAB Code of Ethics be amended to:

   a. include a new clause on human rights making it the responsibility of broadcasters to ensure, to the best of their ability, that their programming contains no abusive or discriminatory material or comment relating to either sex;

b. call upon members to endorse and support the initiatives of the advertising industry in dealing with the issue of sex-role stereotyping and to adhere to the Task Force guidelines on sex-role stereotyping in advertising;

c. include a new clause addressing the issue of sex-role stereotyping; this clause is to state that: "Recognizing that every person has a right to full and equal recognition and to enjoy certain fundamental rights and freedoms, broadcasters shall endeavor to ensure, to the best of their ability, that their programming contains no abusive or discriminatory material or comment which is based on matters of race, national or ethnic origin, color, religion, age, sex, marital status or physical or mental handicap."

2. The Association will also make recommendations to ensure that the language used in programming be of an inclusive nature.

3. For the guidance of all personnel involved in broadcast programming, the Association is developing an educational program dealing with sex-role stereotyping in program production.

4. Radio as well as television members are encouraged to develop specific program material dealing with sex-role stereotyping, which can be part of the CAB program exchange.

5. The Association has embarked on an information program so that the public may be aware of its participation in dealing with sex-role stereotyping.

6. The CAB will hold a workshop on sex-role stereotyping at its next annual meeting, scheduled for Fall 1982.

7. The CAB is establishing a standing committee on sex-role stereotyping, which will serve as an address for the public to write, and as a mechanism to review complaints.

iii. The Advertising Industry

As a consequence of its involvement with the Task Force, the advertising industry has undertaken the following measures:[59]

First, when the Canadian Code of Advertising Standards was amended, a section on taste, opinion, and public decency was included. This section now states, in part, that "advertising should not present demeaning or derogatory portrayals of individuals or groups and should not contain anything likely, in the light of generally prevailing standards, to cause deep or widespread offence. It is recognized, of course, that standards of taste are subjective and vary widely from person to person, and community to community, and are, indeed, subject to constant change."[60]

As a second measure, the following "positive action statements" were developed and adopted by the Task Force as guidelines to encourage a more positive and realistic portrayal of men and women in advertising messages. These guidelines, applying to all commercials appearing over the air on both radio and television, state:

1. Advertising should recognize the changing roles of men and women in today's society and reflect a broad range of occupations for all.

2. Advertising should reflect a contemporary family structure showing men, women, and children as supportive participants in home management and household tasks, and equally as beneficiaries of the positive attributes of family life.

3. Advertising, in keeping with the nature of the market and the product, should reflect the wide spectrum of Canadian life, portraying men and women of various ages, backgrounds, and appearances, actively pursuing a wide range of interests--sports, hobbies, business--as well as home-centered activities.

4. Advertising should reflect the realities of life in terms of the intellectual and emotional equality of the sexes by showing men and women as comparably capable, resourceful, self-confident, intelligent, imaginative, and independent.

5. Advertising should emphasize the positive, personal benefits derived from products or services and avoid portraying any excessive dependence on or excessive need for them.

6. Advertising should not exploit women or men purely for attention-getting purposes. Their presence should be relevant to the advertised product.

7. Advertising should, without going to artificial extremes, employ inclusive, non-sexist terms, for example, "hours" or "working hours" rather than "man hours"; "synthetic" rather than "man-made"; "business executives" rather than "businessmen" or "business-women".

8. Advertising should portray men and women as users, buyers, and decision makers, both for "big

63

ticket" items and major services as well as for smaller items.

9. Advertising should reflect a greater use of women, both as voice-overs and as experts and authorities.

As a third measure, the AAB and COGEP have both established an advisory committee on sex-role stereotyping to receive and process complaints about sex-role stereotyping in advertising, and are developing a program to implement the Task Force advertising guidelines. Brochures have been widely distributed describing the purpose of these committees and specifying mailing addresses for complaints submitted in English and French.

Fourth, as noted earlier in this report, a film called "Women Say The Darndest Things" has been produced. This production is designed to help advertisers and others recognize and understand the problem of sex-role stereotyping. It has been shown at speaking engagements featuring members of the AAB advisory committee on sex-role stereotyping, and is available to interested groups on request.

In addition to these steps, the advertising industry will undertake a national attitude study in order to create benchmarks to measure changes in public perceptions of sex-role stereotyping as well as other issues.

C. Task Force Recommendations

In order to maximize the effectiveness of the self-regulatory programs of the broadcasting and advertising industries, and to ensure effective monitoring of progress made toward the elimination of sex-role stereotyping in the broadcast media, the Task Force offers the following recommendations.

i. To the CRTC

The Task Force on Sex-Role Stereotyping recommends that the CRTC:

1. monitor and assess the initiatives taken by the broadcasting and advertising industries for a period of two years by:

   a. undertaking periodic monitoring of broadcast commercials and programming for sex-role stereotyping;

   b. requesting and assessing interim reports from industry committees responsible for self-regulation;

   c. assessing complaints received both by the Commission and through the response system instituted by the government;

   d. at the end of two years, publishing the results of its findings in a report and creating an appropriate public forum for its discussion prior to the consideration of further action by the Commission;

2. require all licensees to submit periodic reports to the Commission on their progress and initiatives in dealing with the problem of sex-role stereotyping;

3. take initiatives to eliminate abusive comments on, or abusive pictorial representation of, either sex in broadcast content (AM, FM, TV). The Commission

should also discourage the portrayal of gratuitous violence against women;

4. make the report of this Task Force widely available. In particular, it should be distributed to broadcast licensees, women's groups, and to all who made submissions to the Task Force.

ii. To the Federal Government

The Task Force on Sex-Role Stereotyping recommends to the Federal Government that it:

1. accept the principle that programming on the Canadian broadcasting system be reflective of the interest of both sexes;

2. establish and maintain an effective response system, such as a toll-free number or a postage-free mailing system, to receive public complaints about sex-role stereotyping in radio and television programming or commercials, which would supplement the self-regulatory initiatives established by the broadcasting and advertising industries. Records should be maintained indicating the nature of the complaints received and the existence of the system should be widely publicized;

3. encourage and finance the development of a methodology by which progress in the area of sex-role stereotyping in programming and commercials can be measured, and that this work be undertaken or commissioned by an appropriate body, such as Status of Women Canada or the Department of the Secretary of State's Women's Program. Such studies should not duplicate those undertaken by the advertising or broadcasting industries as set out in their proposals for self-regulation;

4. compile and periodically update, either through the Department of the Secretary of State's Women's Program or a comparable body, comprehensive regional and national directories of women experts, to be made available as a resource to any broadcast licensee;

5. note the fact that women are under-represented as members both of the CRTC and the CBC Board of Directors and that this be considered when appointments are made to these publicly-funded agencies, to ensure more balanced representation.

iii. To the Canadian Broadcasting Corporation

The Task Force recognizes that the Canadian Association of Broadcasters has implemented a number of commitments made in response to public concern regarding sex-role stereotyping in its programming.[61] In the interest of achieving further progress, the Task Force recommends that the CBC:

1. ensure that all its programming staff become familiar with, and adhere to, the Corporation's policies and guidelines pertaining to the portrayal of women in programming;

2. undertake, on an annual basis, comparative studies of the portrayal of women on both its English-language and French-language television services, and make the results of these studies available to the public;

3. take into consideration, in all its future studies on women and employment, persons employed by the Corporation on a contract basis.

iv. To the Private Broadcasting Industry

The Task Force recognizes that the Canadian Association of Broadcasters has agreed to establish a standing committee on sex-role stereotyping to receive and process complaints from the public. The CAB has also agreed to develop a program to educate production staff about sex-role stereotyping in broadcast programming. In addition, the CAB's Board of Directors will recommend to the 1982 general meeting of the association that its Code of Ethics be amended to include clauses that will specifically address the issue of sex-role stereotyping in radio and television programming. The association has already embarked on an information program to ensure that the public is aware of its activities in this area.[62]

The Task Force on Sex-Role Stereotyping recommends:

1. that the Canadian Association of Broadcasters adopt, as association policy, the proposed changes to the CAB Code of Ethics, which will be presented to the 1982 CAB annual meeting for approval;

2. that the mandate of the CAB standing committee on sex-role stereotyping include: education; encouraging the cooperation and participation of member stations; handling complaints; and making interim public reports;

3. that the CAB outline to the CRTC how it proposes to educate and sensitize its members with respect to sex-role stereotyping;

4. that the CAB committee encourage members to increase the visibility and involvement of women both on- and off-air;

5. that all CAB-member broadcasters participate in the implementation of the association's proposal for self-regulation, and cooperate in making it effective;

6. that all private broadcasters familiarize themselves with the programming proposals as set up in this report, and adopt the applicable programming recommendations;

7. that all private broadcasters exercise sensitivity to, and awareness of, the problem of sex-role stereotyping in the acquisition of programming material or rights.

v. To the Advertising Industry

As a result of its participation on this Task Force, the advertising industry has undertaken the following activities for the purpose of reducing sex-role stereotyping in broadcast commercials.

First, a set of advertising guidelines pertaining to sex-role stereotyping was developed for use by industry members, and advisory committees on sex-role stereotyping were established under the aegis of both the AAB and the COGEP to receive and process public complaints arising from the guidelines. These committees have also agreed to forward interim reports on all phases of their activities. As well, a film was commissioned for the specific purpose of promoting understanding of the guidelines among advertisers. An information program is in place to inform the public about the committees' activities. The advisory committees will undertake research on public perceptions about issues affecting advertising, including sex-role stereotyping.[63]

The Task Force on Sex-Role Stereotyping recommends that the advertising industry:

1. encourage its members to participate in the implementation of the industry's proposal for self-regulation and cooperate with the industry in making it effective;

2. after gaining experience with the voluntary guidelines and the self-regulation process during the two-year period following the publication of the Task Force report, review, and where appropriate modify, industry codes relating to the portrayal of individuals, notably women, in advertising.

vi. To Other Participants in the Canadian Broadcasting System

While there was no representative on the Task Force either from the newly-licensed pay-TV licensees, the cable television industry, or any of the educational broadcasting authorities, the Task Force, recognizing that they are participants in the Canadian broadcasting system, urges them all to:

1. recognize the public concern about sex-role stereotyping;

2. adopt the applicable programming recommendations set out in this report;

3. exercise sensitivity to, and awareness of, the problem of sex-role stereotyping in the acquisition of programming material or rights where applicable;

4. ensure that women are adequately represented both on- and off-air.

vii. To the Public

First and foremost, the Task Force on Sex-Role
Stereotyping urges the public to make known its
concerns and complaints about what it finds
objectionable in broadcast programming and
commercials.

Appendix 12, Complaints Procedures and Redress
Mechanisms, summarizes the various options available
to a complainant and outlines the redress mechanisms
currently available: the complaint procedures offered
by self-regulatory bodies established by the relevant
industries, and the intervention process available at
public hearings. It includes an index of names and
addresses of organizations to which complaints may be
forwarded. It is hoped, in addition, that the toll-free
number or postage-free mailing system for registering
complaints, recommended by the Task Force, will be
put in place in the near future.

Therefore, when a radio or television program or an
advertising message is objectionable in its
presentation of women, use the avenues that are
available to make your complaint known; only by this
means can your concerns be heard, listened to, and
acted upon.

D. Sex Stereotyping Goes Beyond Broadcasting

The Task Force recognizes that the broadcasting and
advertising industries do not by themselves have a
responsibility for correcting all the injustices caused
by sex-role stereotyping. Many of these reflect the
conflicts concomitant with a society undergoing rapid
change, and in any event it is recognized that these
problems cannot be corrected overnight.

E. The Future

Changes in attitude and awareness of the problem, in the long run, will accomplish more than guidelines. However, guidelines and/or self-regulation are useful, first in bringing attention to the problem, and then in providing an avenue to explore solutions.

Because some of the members of the Task Force were reluctant to give industry the opportunity to address the problem of sex-role stereotyping through self-regulation, the Task Force agreed that the effectiveness of self-regulation should be assessed at the end of two years. When this assessment is completed by the CRTC, industry, and the public sector, guidelines and recommendations for proposed action may need to be updated and changed; indeed, other alternatives may need to be explored.

F. Additional Recommendations by Public Members

While the public members of the Task Force on Sex-Role Stereotyping were in full support of the previous recommendations, and in fact commended the Task Force on the progress that had been made, they offered additional recommendations designed to facilitate the implementation of goals. They expressed concern that issues, plans, and commitments be more specific; and that mechanisms should be put in place which will outlive the particular involvement of the individuals who have participated in this process, who understand the issues and problems, and who made specific commitments for change and progress. In addition, they expressed concern about the importance of accountability, and of a continuing role for the public in this process, since the Task Force existed precisely because of the public in general and women's concerns in particular. To this end, therefore, the public members add the following recommendations.

i. To the CRTC

1. In order to ensure an appropriate mechanism for the CRTC to carry out the tasks of monitoring and assessing the initiatives for self-regulation of the broadcasting and advertising industries, the public members recommend:

> that the CRTC establish a committee on sex-role stereotyping. The mandate of this committee would be as outlined in Recommendation 1 of the Task Force to the CRTC.

And to ensure the continuing involvement of the public, the public members recommend:

> that this committee be composed of CRTC Commissioners and staff, and members of the public familiar with the issues.

2. In order to increase accountability and facilitate public involvement in assessing initiatives and progress, the public members recommend:

> that periodic reports of all licensees on their progress and initiatives in dealing with the problem of sex-role stereotyping be made available to the public at the time of licence renewal.

3. To clarify the meaning and intent of the CRTC's initiatives in eliminating abusive comments or pictorial representations of both sexes, the public members recommend:

> that the CRTC and all licensees recognize the special problems of pornography and violence against women.

Male dominance and female submissiveness are at
the very heart of the stereotypes of men and
women. Pornography is the extreme portrayal of
dominance and the exploitation of women's
sexuality. Pornography, or any portrayal of
violence against women, is the ultimate expression
of dominance/submissiveness, the objectification
and the abuse of women. As such, pornography or
the portrayal of violence against women has no
place in the broadcast media. And as one
mechanism for implementing this, the public
members recommend the following specific
initiatives that the CRTC could undertake:

> that the CRTC amend its AM and FM
> regulations to include, among those subjects
> that may not be broadcast, abusive comments
> on either sex.

And further:

> that the CRTC amend its television regulations
> to include, among those subjects that may not
> be broadcast, abusive comments or abusive
> pictorial representations of either sex.

ii. To the Federal Government

1. As one mechanism for the implementation of the
   recommendation that the federal government
   accept the principle that programming be
   reflective of the interests of both men and women,
   the public members recommend:

> that the Broadcasting Act be amended to
> require that programming provided by the
> Canadian broadcasting system reflect the
> interests of both sexes.

2. With respect to the under-representation of women as members of the publicly-funded CRTC and CBC Board of Directors, the public members recommend:

> that the Government of Canada not only consider the under-representation of women, but also take action to remedy this problem.

Specifically, the public members recommend:

> that half of those individuals appointed to the CRTC and the CBC Board of Directors be women;

and:

> that among individuals next appointed, there should be individuals conversant with problems of sex-role stereotyping and the portrayal of women.

iii. To the Canadian Broadcasting Corporation

In addition to the Task Force's general recommendations to the CBC, the public members put forth the following recommendations:

1. Repeating a recommendation that has been made by women's groups to the CBC since at least 1978, the public members recommend:

> that the CBC Board of Directors institute an on-going advisory committee (made up of representatives of feminist organizations) that would speak specifically on the subject of the portrayal of women on CBC radio and television.

2. To facilitate the implementation of CBC commitments and policies, the public members recommend:

> that CBC departments such as public affairs, drama, sports, children's programming, and so forth, be required to draw up an annual "plan of action" regarding the institution or initiation of positive actions in order to live up to the CBC's policies on the portrayal of women.

The public members further recommend:

> that an annual internal assessment by CBC departments be undertaken to report on and measure, where possible, progress made toward achieving those goals.

And, to demonstrate a clear commitment to the work of this Task Force as well as cooperation with the CRTC's job of assessment, the public members recommend:

> that these reports be submitted as the CBC's interim reports to the CRTC.

3. In order to assure accountability to the CRTC and to the public, the public members recommend:

> that the CBC's periodic monitoring studies be submitted to the CRTC as interim reports, and that these studies be made widely available to the public.

And further:

> that the CBC's interim reports to the CRTC include a summary of all activities and achievements of the Corporation with regard to

the portrayal of women in programming. This
report should include a complete summary of
complaints that the CBC has received
concerning the portrayal of women and the
actions taken in response to these complaints.

4. Finally, because its Equal Opportunity Policy
   applies only to employees of the Corporation, the
   public members recommend that the CBC not only
   assess the situation of persons on contract, as
   specified in Recommendation 3 of the Task Force
   to the CBC, but also:

   that the CBC increase the use of freelance
   women as writers, directors, producers, and so
   forth, in order to ensure a better representation
   of women's perspective.

iv. To the Private Broadcasting Industry

In order to ensure public involvement and
accountability, the public members recommend:

   that the CAB Committee on Sex-Role
   Stereotyping include public representation.

And further:

   that the interim reports of the committee be
   made widely available to the public.

FOOTNOTES

FOREWORD

1. Statistics Canada, "The Labour Force," Cat. No. 71-001, Table 3.

2. Ibid.

3. Statistics Canada, "Historical Labour Force Statistics--Actual Data, Seasonal Factors--Unadjusted Data," Cat. No. 71-201.

4. Idem, "The Labour Force," Cat. No. 71-001, Table 19.

5. Idem, "Income Distributions by Size," 1979, Cat. No. 13-207, Table 71.

6. Idem, "The Labour Force," Cat. No. 71-001, Table 6.

7. Idem, "Income Distributions by Size," 1979, Cat. No. 13-207, Tables 72 and 73.

8. Idem, "Market Research Handbook 1981," Cat. No. 63-224, Tables 4-10.

9. Idem, "The Estimates of Population by Sex and Age for Canada," Cat. No. 91-Z02.

CHAPTER 1

10. The National Plan of Action on the Status of Women is outlined in Towards Equality for Women/Femmes en voie d'égalité (Ottawa: Supply and Services Canada, 1979).

11. See Appendix 1, Sex Stereotyping in the Media: Address by the Honourable David MacDonald, Department of the Secretary of State of Canada, to the Institute of Canadian Advertising, 28 September 1979.

12. Details of these submissions are given in Appendix 2, Submissions to the Task Force by Organizations and/or Individuals.

13. This documentation forms the bibliography of this report.

CHAPTER 2

14. Nova Scotia Status of Women, Herself, Status of Women Task Force Report (1976), quoted in: Nova Scotia Human Rights Commission, Women and Advertising (Nova Scotia: The Commission, 1979), p. 1.

15. National Council of Welfare, Women and Poverty (Ottawa: The Council, 1979), p. 22.

16. Research on the social effects of sex stereotyping in advertising is detailed in: A. Courtney and T. Whipple, Canadian Perspectives on Sex Stereotyping in Advertising (Ottawa: Advisory Council on the Status of Women, 1978).

CHAPTER 3

17. Montréal YWCA, Sexism and Advertising, Report of the Committee on Sexism and Advertising (Montréal: YWCA, December 1978).

18. Nova Scotia Human Rights Commission, Women and Advertising, p. 58.

19. Federation of Women Teachers' Associations of Ontario, Women in Crisis, Report of the Ad Hoc Committee on Problems of Women in Crisis (Toronto: The Federation, March 1981).

20. As the body charged with regulation of broadcasting in Canada, the CRTC receives complaints on a great variety of matters related to broadcasting through both the public hearing process and letters. In the past few years, several major interventions have been made before the CRTC at network licence renewal hearings on the subject of sex-role stereotyping.

21. See Appendix 2, Submissions to the Task Force by Organizations and/or Individuals.

22. Names of advertisers, programs, stations, or networks have been deleted. Complete texts from which the excerpts are taken are available on request by contacting Information Services, CRTC, Ottawa, Ontario K1A 0N2 either in writing or by telephoning (819) 997-0313.

23. This quotation is taken from a brief, which was presented to a public meeting of the Task Force in Montréal on 4 February 1980, and entitled "La représentation du corps dans la publicité," ("The Representation of the Body in Publicity") in Anthropologica, N.S. vol. XXI, no. 1, 1979). Further quotations from Annie Méar are from the same brief.

24. Here, the Women's Liaison Committee is quoting from Lucy Komisar, "The Image of Women in Advertising," in Women in Sexist Society: Studies in Power and Powerlessness (New York: Basic Books, 1971).

25. All quotations by the Réseau d'action et d'information pour les femmes are taken from a paper presented at the Seminar on the Image of Women organized by the CBC in February 1979 and attached to a letter to the Task Force.

26. March 8 is International Women's Day (editor's note).

CHAPTER 4

27. The Task Force regrets that, although it received submissions on the merits of advertising feminine hygiene products, its mandate did not permit it to address this issue.

CHAPTER 5

28. See Appendix 3, Government of Québec Advertising Guidelines.

29. These policies, and the set of English-language guidelines, are reproduced in Appendix 4, CBC Submission to the CRTC Task Force on Sex-Role Stereotyping.

30. See Appendix 5, Canadian Association of Broadcasters, section A, Canadian Association of Broadcasters Code of Ethics.

31. See Appendix 4, CBC Submission to the CRTC Task Force on Sex-Role Stereotyping, Addendum 4, CBC Commercial Acceptance Policy Directive, 12 June 1980: CBC Standards of Good Taste.

32. La Confédération générale de la publicité (COGEP) and le Conseil des normes de la publicité are the equivalent, for French-speaking communities across Canada, of the Advertising

Advisory Board (AAB, formerly Canadian
Advisory Board) and the Advertising
Standards Council. Since November 1981,
matters of policy and financing of these four
organizations are the responsibility of the
Canadian Advertising Foundation.

33.   See Appendix 6, The Advertising Industry, section
      B, Canadian Code of Advertising Standards.

34.   See Appendix 4, Addendum 6, Equal Opportunity
      of Employment Policy. This policy was first
      developed by the CBC in 1975.

CHAPTER 6

35.   See Appendix 5, Canadian Association of
      Broadcasters, section B, Sex-Role Stereotyping
      Report of the Canadian Association of
      Broadcasters.

36.   In the case of advertising, the Canadian
      Advertising Advisory Board (now the Advertising
      Advisory Board) provided the original impetus
      when the results of a pilot test comparing
      "liberated" and "traditional" commercials
      underwritten in 1977 by its Task Force on Women
      In Advertising revealed "that liberated advertising
      is more likely to be effective than traditional
      advertising." The study concluded that, "from the
      advertising effectiveness point of view, the real
      issue is not whether to be liberated, but how to be
      liberated without being irritating." This led the
      CAAB to recommend that advertisers ensure that
      women who work outside the home be included in
      market pre-testing of commercials (currently
      being done by some advertisers). Accounts of this
      pilot test are found in the following: The
      Canadian Advertising Advisory Board,

Women and Advertising, Today's Messages--
Yesterday's Images? Report of the Task Force on
Women and Advertising (Toronto: CAAB,
November 1977), p.18; and A. Courtney and T.
Whipple, Canadian Perspectives on Sex
Stereotyping in Advertising (Ottawa: Canadian
Advisory Council on the Status of Women, June
1978).

37. These arguments were based on the results of a
    monitoring study by the intervenors on CBC
    program content, an analysis of which was
    presented as part of the joint brief.

38. These were l'Association de femmes de Radio-
    Canada, la Fédération des femmes du Québec, the
    Federated Women's Institutes of Canada, the
    National Action Committee on the Status of
    Women, le Réseau d'action et d'information pour
    les femmes, and the Vancouver Status of Women.

39. These commitments are outlined in Appendix 4,
    Addendum 2, Portrayal of Women in CBC
    Programming.

40. "The Presence, Role and Image of Women in
    Prime Time on the English Television Network of
    the CBC", and "The Presence, Role and Image of
    Women in Prime Time on the French Television
    Network of the CBC", reports submitted by the
    Office of the Co-ordinator, Portrayal of Women
    (Ottawa: CBC, 1982).

41. The CBC plans to monitor categories of its
    programming on a cyclical basis.

42. The CBC task force recommended that a separate
    examination of the pay of contract personnel be
    conducted. Five steps were suggested for this
    study: first, a collection of data on pay practices

and fees actually paid to men and women for doing the same or similar work; second, identification of apparent anomalies; third, follow-up to determine the underlying facts; fourth, estimation of the extent of discrimination; and last, recommendation of corrective action, if required. No action was taken on these recommendations.

43. See Appendix 4, Addendum 5, CBC Task Force on the Status of Women: Recommendations and Implementation, January 1981.

44. See Appendix 4, Addendum 5.

45. As mentioned in section i of this chapter under the commitments and actions taken by the CBC, responsibility for coordinating the CBC's commitments in the area of broadcast commercials is exercised by the Coordinator, Portrayal of Women in Programming.

46. See Appendix 4, Addendum 4, CBC Commercial Acceptance Policy Directive. This subject is also treated in Chapter 5, Government Regulation and Industry Self-regulation, section B.ii.

47. Maxene Raices, "Male and Female Roles in OECA Programming," OECA Office of Project Research, Report No. 13 (Toronto: OECA, September 1976).

48. See Appendix 5, Canadian Association of Broadcasters, section B, Sex-Role Stereotyping Report of the Canadian Association of Broadcasters.

49. The recommendations of the CAAB Task Force on Women and Advertising are included in Appendix 6, The Advertising Industry, section A.

50. The Canadian Advertising Advisory Board, <u>Women and Advertising, Today's Messages - Yesterday's Images</u>? Report of the Task Force on Women and Advertising (Toronto: CAAB, November 1977).

51. See Appendix 6, The Advertising Industry, section B, Canadian Code of Advertising Standards.

52. See Appendix 6, The Advertising Industry, section C, Advertising Industry Brief to the CRTC Task Force on Sex-Role Stereotyping.

53. The nine positive action statements are reproduced in Appendix 6, section C.ii. The Positive Portrayal of the Sexes in Broadcast Advertising.

CHAPTER 7

54. The implementation of commitments made by the CBC, before the Task Force was established, is reviewed in Chapter 6, section B, Broadcasting Industry Responses, part i. The Canadian Broadcasting Corporation, under "Programming."

55. This is detailed in Chapter 6, section B.i. The Canadian Broadcasting Corporation.

56. "The Presence, Role and Image of Women in Prime Time on the English Television Network of the CBC," and "The Presence, Role and Image of Women in Prime Time on the French Television Network of the CBC", reports submitted by the Office of the Co-ordinator, Portrayal of Women (Ottawa: CBC, 1982). See also Chapter 6, section B.i. The Canadian Broadcasting Corporation, under "Programming." Copies of these reports are available from the CBC Information Centre, 1500 Bronson Avenue, Ottawa, Ontario, K1G 3J5.

57. This subject is reviewed in Chapter 6, section B.i.
     Broadcast Commercials.

58. This is outlined in greater detail in Chapter 6,
     section B.iii. The Private Broadcasting Industry.
     As much as possible, the CAB measures given
     here are reproduced in their original form.

59. This is given in greater detail in Chapter 6, under
     section B.iv. The Advertising Industry.

60. See also Appendix 6, The Advertising Industry,
     section B, Canadian Code of Advertising
     Standards.

61. This subject is reviewed in Chapter 6, section B.i.
     The Canadian Broadcasting Corporation, under
     "Programming".

62. All of the above issues are discussed in detail in
     Chapter 6, section B.iii. The Private
     Broadcasting Industry. Further, the CAB's
     decisions following its participation on the Task
     Force are outlined in the present chapter, section
     B, Task Force Achievements, in part ii. The
     Private Broadcasting Industry.

63. For more detail on the activities of the
     advertising industry and the steps that led to the
     formation of the advisory committees, see
     Chapter 6, under section B.iv. The Advertising
     Industry. See also section B of the present
     chapter, on Task Force Achievements, part iii.
     The Advertising Industry.

APPENDIX 1

SEX STEREOTYPING IN THE MEDIA: Address by the Honourable David Macdonald, Department of the Secretary of State of Canada, to the Institute of Canadian Advertising, 28 September 1979

Since becoming a member of the Cabinet in June, I have given speeches at different times wearing one of my different hats--I have spoken as Secretary of State, or as Minister responsible for the Status of Women, or as Minister of Communications.

What is unique about my speaking to you here today is that, in addressing the problem of sex-stereotyping in advertising in the electronic media, I can speak wearing any, or all, of my hats. This issue is of concern to me from the point of view of Minister of Communications responsible for the CRTC, as Secretary of State responsible for the CBC, and as Minister responsible for the Status of Women, since, when we are talking about sex-stereotyping in the media, we are talking mostly about how our advertisers and broadcasters portray women.

Recently, an eight-year-old acquaintance, on discovering that in her mother's day, girls could not be on the school patrol (they were "patrol boys" then), exclaimed in exasperation, "Sometimes I wonder what boys think girls are!" A good question--and one that, unless things change at lightning pace, this little girl will be asking for a long time to come. And if that little girl watches television (and doesn't escape for peanut butter sandwiches during the commercials), she might ask, "Sometimes I wonder what men think women are."

She herself has a fairly good idea of what women are. She has a mother who goes out to work, who comes home with a briefcase full of files and who, more often than not, forgets to mop the floor. When her mother gets together with friends, they talk about politics, literature, or sports. The little girl herself wants to be a writer, an architect, or a politician. These are the images that she has of women. And yet she turns on the TV and is bombarded with images of women in the kitchen (scrubbing the floor); in the bathroom (scrubbing the sink); in the laundry room (scrubbing the stubborn stains from hubby's shirt). When she isn't scrubbing, she's talking about the joy and satisfaction of the clean floor, the clean sink, the clean shirt! And when she gets together with other women, they compare notes about how to best clean the floor, the sink, the shirt!

Given this barrage of images from the television screen (and we haven't even touched on the images projected in the programs themselves), the little girl might begin to change her question to: "Is this what women are supposed to be?" Then she'll ask, "What's wrong with me?" and gradually, her dreams of being a writer, architect, or politician will fade.

Is this an exaggeration? I don't think that it is. This audience is more aware than the average citizen about the power of advertising--and the power of the images that advertising projects. Thomas Whipple and Alice Courtney, who have done much work in this field, know about the power of those images as well. In a paper on the social consequences of sex stereotyping, they state:

> The effect of stereotyping on children is the best researched of any of the areas. There now is evidence to indicate that the aspirations and levels of achievement of boys and girls are influenced by their perceptions of the roles of the sexes. There also is evidence to show that advertising is a contributor to the sex-role perceptions held by children. Thus, advertising influences the sexual socialization of children and

may contribute to determination of their life styles, choices of education and occupation, and marital role.

I don't think there's much doubt that the images portrayed in advertising have an effect on the socialization of both children and adults. That's why advertising is a multi-million dollar business. If advertising were not an effective method of inducing the public to desire (and buy) products, corporations wouldn't spend money on it, and advertising agencies wouldn't exist.

Given this, what makes the kind of stereotyping of women that is prevalent in advertising (and programming) ... so insidious, is that it is not reflecting the reality of woman's role today; and, as a result, the image that it is passing on to the population is a distortion. It is, in effect, telling the little girl a lie about herself and her possibilities. That is the problem with sex stereotyping in advertising today: it is not projecting a true (or even nearly true) image of women; and yet, the image that it does project is one that is believed by many people, and one on which they base their decisions and their actions.

How can women expect to break into non-traditional jobs--such as plumber or welder--when the image of woman that is projected from the radio, the television, newspapers, movies, magazines, is one of a delicate and fragile creature in high heels and a low-cut dress? How can a woman convince the corporate executive that she would make an excellent manager, when he has spent most of his life absorbing images of women who need a man to balance the check book and to tell them what insurance is?

According to the report done by Courtney and Whipple for the Advisory Council on the Status of Women:

91

Advertising becomes one of the factors that causes individual women to limit their access to various occupations and influences society itself to limit women's access to those occupations. This phenomenon has both social and economic effects, including the "ghettoization" of female work, with its related effect on salaries for women.

The problem is a serious one. Since 1971, there have been more than 30 monitoring studies on the portrayal of women in advertising. These studies show that women are portrayed, for the most part, as housewives and mothers, dependent upon men and subservient to them. They are shown as compulsive consumers, devoting their lives to buying products to keep their husbands and children happy. When not playing the consuming-nurturing role, they play the sex-object role --either as decoration in advertisements directed to men, or as dumb-but-beautiful, adorning themselves with a myriad of products to make them attractive to men. The fact that almost 50 per cent of all women are in the work force; that 46 per cent of married women work outside the home; that, of all women in the labor force, close to one-half are not married and many of those support dependents themselves--these facts are seldom reflected in advertisements, either in the print or electronic media.

The result is what one writer on the subject, Rena Bartos, in the Harvard Business Review, has called a "reality gap." She goes on to say that "changes in women's lives may be the missing factor in many marketing programs and may result in unrealized potential and lost opportunities." Thus, not only are advertisers insulting women with the images they project, but they may even be damaging their own business. This is a fact that is perhaps beginning to dawn on the advertising industry, since both the

Canadian Advertising Advisory Board, and the National Advertising Review Board in the U.S., have recognized that their portrayal of women is turning off a large chunk of their audience. As the Report on Advertising and Women prepared by NARB puts it:

> It would appear that the more vocal critics of advertising as "sexist" are younger, better educated, more articulate women who often are opinion leaders. On the average they have more discretionary income. As their numbers increase ... their challenge to advertising will probably become greater, unless constructive action is taken.

That was written in 1975. The CAAB's report was written in 1977. And yet the same old images persist.

You might ask, why don't women complain. The fact is that they do complain, but ... there has been no mechanism set up to deal with their complaints. The Canadian Code of Advertising Standards, administered by the CAAB, does not include any reference to sex stereotyping, nor to insulting portrayal of the sexes. In fact, the CAAB has consistently maintained that issues concerning the portrayal of women fall into the category of "taste and opinion," and are thus specifically omitted from the class of complaints that will be dealt with. Thus, women would be discouraged from making any complaints to the Advertising Standards Council.

But when women are asked to air their views about advertising (as they were five years ago by the Ontario Status of Women Council), they do not mince their words. Here are a few examples of what women think about how they are portrayed on television:

"In my opinion almost all TV ads make women appear as fools, interested only in their wash or their breath!"

"The all-too-prevalent notion of males 'doing business' contrasted with the insipid, necessarily-content-in-the-kitchen female ... is disgustingly insulting to women, even those married to their kitchen!"

A well-known ad that shows a family group on a sailboat and ends saying, "After all, we brought Mom along," brought this comment from an angry respondent: "Mom sounds like the family dog."

The women who responded to the Ontario Status of Women Council survey were, almost without exception, angry, disgusted, and insulted by the portrayal of women in TV advertising. The angry response of one sums up the whole problem: "Women just don't carry on that way. Advertisers must have a low opinion about women to put this garbage on the air"--which takes us back to our eight-year-old's question about just what boys think girls are.

Given the almost unanimous condemnation of the portrayal of women in advertising by the women to whom the ads (for the most part) are addressed, one wonders why advertisers continue presenting the negative stereotypes. One argument used is that, if women were really so upset by advertisements, they would refuse to buy the products. This ignores the fact that women have little choice--all the detergent ads present the same negative image, but the woman still has to buy soap! The same goes for toothpaste and other essentials. Women have little choice about what they buy.

It would appear, however, that advertisers have a choice about how they sell. The results of a CAAB survey on "liberated" advertising showed that liberated (or non-sexist ads) are "at least equal to, and possibly more effective than, more traditional advertising approaches. All liberated advertisements tested in the pilot research scored higher than their traditional counterparts on several measures of advertising effectiveness." The CAAB report goes on to say that "the real issue is not whether to be liberated, but rather how to be liberated without being irritating" (i.e. exaggerated or unrealistic). How to do it is a question you as advertisers must work out. That you should be doing it is, from my point of view (wearing my three hats) beyond question. That you are not doing it is the impression of the many women and women's groups who have been monitoring the situation over the past decade.

The government does not want to tell advertisers what to say or what to show in their attempt to sell products through advertising. But when that advertising is offensive and insulting to one-half of the population, and when the effect of that advertising is, in fact, to limit the choices and the opportunities of that half of the population, then it is time for the government to bring the problem out in the open and to say to the advertising industry, "What are you going to do about this problem?"

This is, in effect, what I am asking the CRTC to do. Under the chairmanship of Marianne Barrie of St. Thomas, Ontario, the CRTC is setting up a Task Force composed of representatives from the advertising and broadcast industries, from the public, and from the CRTC. The public representatives will be women who have done much work in the area of sex stereotyping:

Jane Hughes of Toronto, managing editor of
Homemaker's magazine, who has coordinated the
program for this afternoon;

Sylvia Spring of Vancouver, a journalist and active
member of the Vancouver Status of Women;

Maria Eriksen of Calgary, a psychologist and
founding member of the Alberta Status of Women
Action Committee;

Lynn McDonald, President of the National Action
Committee on the Status of Women;

Stella Baudot of Montréal, a member of the
Fédération des femmes du Québec and the
Consultative Committee of the Status of Women;

Beth Percival of Charlottetown, President of the
P.E.I. Advisory Council and President of the
Canadian Research Institute for the Advancement
of Women.

The Task Force will hold meetings in Ottawa as well as
regional meetings across the country. Its purpose will
be to delineate guidelines for a more positive (and
realistic) portrayal of women in radio and television (in
both programming and commercials), and to make
policy recommendations for consideration by the
Commission and the broadcast industry.

The Task Force could propose one of several
mechanisms for the implementation of the guidelines it
sets up: industry self-regulation, CRTC regulation, or
government legislation. Which route will be the most
effective will be up to the Task Force to decide. It is
hoped that their work will be completed by the Spring
of next year.

The information I have received from the CRTC is that
the idea of the Task Force has been well received in
both the advertising and the broadcast industries. This
suggests to me that the problem of sex stereotyping is
now being perceived by these industries as a serious
issue. I do hope that this is the case, and that the work
of the Task Force will go a long way to resolving this
issue, which affects not only the role of women, but the
role of men in our changing society.

It has not been my intention today to lay the blame of
sex stereotyping entirely on the advertising industry or
on this audience, as its representatives. In portraying
women as they do, advertisers are reflecting the
stereotypes they see around them, and have seen all
their lives--from the textbooks they read in school
many years ago to the magazines or newspaper they
read last night. A vicious circle is created whereby one
stereotype feeds on another. But the circle has to end
somewhere, and if the advertisers are not responsible
for the stereotypes of women that exist today, they are
responsible to a large extent for the perpetuation of
those stereotypes. Or, put in another and more positive
way, a concerted effort by the advertising industry
would go a long way to ending the vicious circle of the
negative stereotyping of women.

I hope that you, as advertisers, will take up the
challenge that is being offered to you by the CRTC
Task Force, and work together to find a way of selling
products through a positive portrayal of women, in line
with the changing realities of women's lives--in a way
that will show to your daughters, and all our daughters,
that boys (and men) see girls (and women) as equals and
as persons.

97

APPENDIX 2

SUBMISSIONS TO THE TASK FORCE BY ORGANIZATIONS AND/OR INDIVIDUALS

A. Submissions Made at Public Meetings

On 24 January 1980, the Task Force announced a series of public meetings at which interested parties were invited to present and discuss their views on sex-role stereotyping. Presentations were limited to fifteen minutes in length.

The places and dates of the public meetings follow, with a list of submissions heard at each session.

1. Montréal, Québec
   Le Méridien
   4 Complexe Desjardins
   4 February 1980, 7:30 p.m.

Submissions were made by the following organizations and individuals:

i. Organizations

Le Conseil du statut de la femme du Québec, le Comité pour la publicité non-sexiste (Catherine Lord) Montréal YWCA, le Comité sur la publicité et le sexisme (Ginette Busque, Chantal Leduc)

ii. Individuals

Fabienne Mercier
Andréa Martinez

2. Hull, Québec
   Conference Centre
   Phase IV
   140 Promenade du Portage
   11 February 1980, 7:30 p.m.

Submissions were made by the following organizations and individuals:

i. Organizations

Rape Crisis Centre and the Women's Career Counselling Service (Lorraine Manley)

ii. Individuals

Rosemary Kness
Eileen Saunders

3.   Halifax, Nova Scotia
      Citadel Inn
      1900 Brunswick Street
      20 February 1980, 7:30 p.m.

Submissions were made by the following organizations and individuals:

i. Organizations

A Woman's Place, Forest House (Karen Irving-Judd)
Canadian Research Institute for the Advancement of Women (M. Duckworth)
Halifax YWCA, Social Issues Committee (Leslie Sanson, Margaret Vigneault)
Mount Saint Vincent University (Dr. Susan Clark)
Nova Scotia Advisory Council on the Status of Women (Nadine Boudreau)
Nova Scotia Human Rights Commission (George F. McCurdy)
St. Mary's University Women's Caucus (Dr. Gillian Thomas, Dr. Wendy Katz)

ii. Individuals

Joan Fraser
Joanne Greene
Catherine Logan
Judith Wouk

4. Vancouver, British Columbia
    900 West Georgia Street
    20 February 1980, 7:30 p.m.

Submissions were made by the following organizations and individuals:

i. Organizations

British Columbia Teachers' Federation, Status of Women (Maureen McDonald)
Children's Television Association (Donna Bond-Christenson)
Canadian Research Institute for the Advancement of Women (Joan Wallace)
Rape Relief (Joanie Miller)
Satellite Video Exchange Society (Pat Feindel, Shawn Preus)
University of British Columbia, Women Students' Office (Lorette Woolsey)
Vancouver Status of Women (Jillian Ridington)
Women Against Violence Against Women (Susan Moore) and Women in Focus (Marion Barling)

ii. Individuals

Howard Broomfield
Betty-Ann Buss
Dorothy Holme
Robin Ridington

5.   Edmonton, Alberta
     Edmonton Plaza
     10135-100th Street
     4 March 1980, 7:30 p.m.

Submissions were made by the following organizations and individuals:

i. Organizations

Alberta Status of Women Action Committee
(Natalie Maclean)
Calgary YWCA, Social Issues Committee (Phylis Berck, Levan Dubois)
Catholic Women's League, Edmonton Diocese
(Mitzie Crowe)
Edmonton Women's Shelter Ltd. Board (Ruth Whaley)
McIntyre Lewis Advertising (Donald W. McIntyre, Wendy Bittner)
University Women's Club of Edmonton
(Dr. Murina Baur, Dr. Jean Lauber, Tammy Irwin)

ii. Individuals

Jo Evans
Ruth Fraser
Don Herrington
Brenda Manasse
Marilyn Radcliffe
Karen Romans

6.   Toronto, Ontario
     Hotel Toronto
     145 Richmond Street West
     5 March 1980, 7:30 p.m.

Submissions were made by the following individuals and organizations:

i. Organizations

Association of Canadian Advertisers (J.J. McHardy)
Canadian Housewives' Register, Executive Board
(Janet McPate)
Canadian Housewives' Register, Willowdale Group
(Margaret Hilton)
Feminist Party of Canada (Diane Smith)
National Council of Women of Canada (Ruth Jarmain
and Amy Williams)
Ontario Federation of Women Teachers (Ada Hill,
Betty Hawke, Margaret Gee)
Ontario Ministry of Labour, Women's Bureau
(Marnie Clarke)
Political Lesbians United about the Media (Gay Bell)
Status of Women Teachers' Committee, Region 3
(Judy Allison)
Toronto Board of Education, Women's Liaison
Committee (Judy Swartzen)

ii. Individuals

Thea Caplan

B. Submissions Made by Mail

On 28 November 1979, the Task Force invited written
submissions from the public, which, as much as possible,
were to focus on specific recommendations for the
resolution of the problem of sex-role stereotyping. The
deadline for such submissions was 31 January 1980, to
be sent to the care of the CRTC.

The following associations and corporations sent
submissions:

Alberta Action for Responsible Television Association
L'Association féminine d'éducation et d'action sociale
(AFEAS--Cercle de la Providence)

L'Association féminine d'éducation et d'action sociale (AFEAS--Siège social)
Association of Canadian Advertisers, Inc.
British Columbia Teachers' Federation
Calgary Status of Women Action Committee
Canada Packers Ltd.
Canadian Advisory Council on the Status of Women
Canadian Committee on Hearing Opportunities for Women (B.C./Yukon)
Canadian Federation of University Women, Head Office
Canadian Federation of University Women, Kingston Club
Canadian Federation of University Women, Stratford
Canadian Girls in Training, National Association
Canadian Home Economics Association
Canadian Imperial Bank of Commerce
Canadian University Press
Coopérative régionale des consommateurs de Sainte-Foy
Cranbrook Women's Resource Group
Crown Life Insurance Company
Edmonton YWCA
Federation of Women Teachers' Associations of Ontario
General Mills Canada Ltd.
Greb Shoes Inc.
Grocery Products Manufacturers of Canada
Hershey Chocolate of Canada
Kay Livingston Visible Minority Women's Society (Nova Scotia)
Kellogg Salada Canada Ltd.
Manitoba Action Committee on the Status of Women
MATRIX (St. Catharines, Ontario)
Montréal YWCA
National Action Committee on the Status of Women
National Association of Women and the Law, Dalhousie Caucus
National Council of Jewish Women, Toronto Section
National Council of Women of Canada

Nelson-Trail and District Labour Council
North Bay Women's Centre
Nova Scotia Human Rights Commission
Nova Scotia Women's Action Committee
Ontario Coalition of Rape Crisis Centres
Port Coquitlam Area Women's Centre
Prince Edward Island Advisory Council on the Status of Women
Quaker Oats Company of Canada Ltd.
Radio Telefis Eireann
Réseau d'action et d'information pour les femmes (RAIF)
Saskatchewan Advisory Council on the Status of Women
Saskatchewan Labour, Women's Division
Schulz Productions
Seagram Distillers Ltd.
TMX Canada Ltd.
United Church of Canada, Saskatchewan Conference, Media Committee
University Women's Club of Coquitlam, Canadian Federation of University Women
University Women's Club of Edmonton, Education Study Group
Vancouver Status of Women
Warner-Lambert Canada Ltd.
William Neilson Ltd.
Women in Focus, Women Against Violence Against Women
Women's Institute of Nova Scotia
Women's Resource Centre (The Peterborough Women's Committee)
Winnipeg YWCA
Yamaha Motor Canada Ltd.

The following individuals sent submissions:

A. D'Alquen (Edmonton, Alberta)
Merlin Andrew (Toronto, Ontario)
Diana Bacon (Edmonton, Alberta)

Sally M. Bailes (Lennoxville, Québec)
Mardi Bastow (Manuels, Newfoundland)
Kate Beard (Burnaby, British Columbia))
Danielle Beauchamp (petition with 27 signatures)
(Calgary, Alberta)
T.R. Belton (Drayton Valley, Alberta)
Réjeanne Bergeron (St-Hyacinthe, Québec)
Maribeth L. Bird (Belleville, Ontario)
Sylvia Chesworth (Golden, British Columbia)
Olive Clark (Hantsport, Nova Scotia)
Linda Coldwell (Digby, Nova Scotia)
Barbara Eifler (North Vancouver, British Columbia)
Marian L. Fahlenbock (Ancaster, Ontario)
Margaret Fern (Saskatoon, Saskatchewan)
Theresa Flynn (Hamilton, Ontario)
K. Foster (Winnipeg, Manitoba)
Garth E. Garner (Toronto, Ontario)
Juliette Gill (Victoria, British Columbia)
Hertha Giroux (Edmonton, Alberta)
Dorothy Groves (Calgary, Alberta)
R. Hammer (Vancouver, British Columbia)
Helen Hayek (Winnipeg, Manitoba)
Carole Henry, Louise Gravel, Mireille Despard, Hélène
Cabana, and Martin Dufresne (Montréal, Québec)
Diana Hoare (Abbotsford, British Columbia)
Dorothy Holme (Coquitlam, British Columbia)
Sandra Huisman (Edmonton, Alberta)
Betty Jeffries (Courtenay, British Columbia)
Prabha Khosla (Vancouver, British Columbia)
Corinne Kirton (Winnipeg, Manitoba)
Kim Lascelle (Chilliwack, British Columbia)
Mable Leith (Virden, Manitoba)
G.C. Leonard (Mississauga, Ontario)
Linda Levesque (Regina, Saskatchewan)
Rowland Lorimer (Burnaby, British Columbia)
Stephannie MacLeod, Judy Roberts, Diana Roberts, and
Helen MacNeil (Iona, Nova Scotia)
Helen Manning (North Bay, Ontario)

Christiane Marais (Regina, Saskatchewan)
B.M. McKee (Sidney, British Columbia)
Helen Monks (Coquitlam, British Columbia)
Ruth Morison (Mississauga, Ontario)
Heinrich Murken (Hamilton, Ontario)
Jeanne Murphy (petition with 10 signatures (Victoria,
British Columbia)
Amelia Murray (Logan Lake, British Columbia)
Sheila Needham (Kingston, Ontario)
Patricia Newton (North Vancouver, British Columbia)
Irene M. Nickerson (North Bay, Ontario)
Janice L. Noble (Victoria, British Columbia)
Jocelyn Petit (Lasalle, Québec)
Juliette Proom (North Vancouver, British Columbia)
Vera Radio (Vancouver, British Columbia) (sic)
Robin Ridington (Vancouver, British Columbia)
Marie Rochette (Victoriaville, Québec)
E.A. Roncarelli (Toronto, Ontario)
Mary Sands (Moncton, New Brunswick)
Carole Sharp (Brandon, Manitoba)
Christina Simmons, Bruce Tucker (Halifax, Nova Scotia)
Emily Sion (Vancouver, British Columbia)
Denise Sirois (Montréal, Québec)
Marjorie Stone (North Bay, Ontario)
Gail Storey (Vancouver, British Columbia)
R.M. Tarry (Eldorado, Saskatchewan)
Pauline Thompson (Swan Hills, Alberta)
Margaret Turner (Flesherton, Ontario)
Danielle Vézina (Hull, Québec)
H. Jane Wakefield (Calgary, Alberta)

APPENDIX 3

GOVERNMENT OF QUÉBEC ADVERTISING GUIDELINES

1. Discrimination, in this context, means an unfavourable comparison or distinction that is made between two groups of individuals. (This definition is based on the one in the Robert Dictionary, the idea of discrimination being the act of defining, of distinguishing, of separating.)

2. "Discriminatory advertising" is all advertising that affects human dignity by presenting people as inferior, or by demeaning them, in any of the areas listed in clause 3.

3. Discrimination appears primarily in the areas of race, color, sex, sexual orientation, civil status, religion, political convictions, language, ethnic or national origin, social status, age, and mental or physical handicap.

   Sexual discrimination (or sexism) is a belittling or demeaning distinction made between the sexes.

   However, the different definitions of sexism in general use indicate that women are the victims of this form of discrimination.

   The following clauses have been drawn up to improve the image of women without disparaging men.

4. Neither men nor women should be treated in such a way as to be reduced to a decorative or sexual object. In this context, a decoration is any added element, used for no other reason than to embellish, bearing no relationship to the normal use of the product. (By "product" is meant an article, a service or a message of public interest.)

107

5. Neither men nor women should be gratuitously presented as weak or inferior, or unduly dependent physically or emotionally upon the other.

6. Neither men nor women should be presented in a manner that belittles intellectual capacities.

7. Equality of the sexes must be reflected in the attributes that characters portrayed in advertising are made to possess. To this end, advertising must not:

    a. attribute certain physical qualities to one sex more than to the other;

    b. present the use of a product as apt to confer, in its own right, the power of seduction.

8. Equality of the sexes must also be reflected by the division of social and parental roles.

    To this end, advertising must:

    a. avoid systematically associating certain types of products with only one sex when these products are used by both men and women;

    b. show that a diversity of careers is equally accessible to both men and women;

    c. tend to show both men and women as equally responsible for domestic tasks, and for the education and care of children;

    d. eliminate servile attitudes.

9. Where children are concerned, advertising must not habitually associate a product or a service with one sex to the exclusion of the other.

108

10. Advertising should try to use a fair balance of both men and women for off-camera voices in order to reflect the principle of equality of the sexes.

11. Advertising must not, in its use of animals or objects personifying human beings, contravene the preceding clause.

APPENDIX 4

CBC SUBMISSION TO THE CRTC TASK FORCE ON SEX-ROLE STEREOTYPING

May 1981 - This document, prepared at the request of the CRTC Task Force on Sex-Role Stereotyping in the broadcast media, includes: a review of the main steps taken by the CBC to improve the portrayal of women on the air; a list of our commitments; and a summary of the efforts made to ensure that those commitments are honored. We have also added a section on our policies concerning equal opportunity.

A. Portrayal of Women

Although the subject of the portrayal of women on the air is not new to the CBC, the CRTC licence renewal hearings of 1978 marked the turning point.

During these hearings, six women's groups representative of the whole country made their dissatisfaction known. In particular, they objected to the stereotyped images of women projected in programming and in commercials. They also deplored the absence of women in news and public affairs programs, both as program personnel and as subject matter.

CBC President A.W. Johnson responded immediately by undertaking before the CRTC to set up a two-day seminar to which representatives of the women's organizations would be invited to discuss specifically the questions raised by their submissions to the CRTC. Mr. Johnson made it clear that he was making this commitment along with his senior colleagues. (See Addendum 1. Excerpts from the Transcripts of the 1978 CRTC Hearings.)

110

i. Commitments

This seminar was held on February 22 and 23, 1979, and after long and useful discussions, CBC Management made the following commitments:

- to develop a program policy on portrayal of women in CBC programs;

- to develop guidelines to eliminate sexist bias and language;

- to establish a process of program evaluation to monitor implementation of objectives;

- to establish a "social affairs specialist" in TV news for the English and French networks to ensure comprehensive coverage of issues of concern to women;

- to develop awareness sessions on sex-role stereotyping and sexist imagery for production staff.

- in commercials:

    - to encourage the CRTC to discuss sexism in advertising;

    - to analyze commercials aired on the networks with a view to articulating the norms and standards that should be established for the industry as a whole;

    - to review promotional material.

- to host a follow-up meeting in one year to assess the effectiveness of the measures agreed upon and to hold periodic informal consultations.

- For details on equal opportunity commitment see section on equal opportunity.

Since then, events have moved swiftly.

ii. Implementation

a. Programming: A program policy has been promulgated which requires the CBC to accept as part of its mandate the need to reflect in its programs the role of women in Canadian society. (See Addendum 2. Portrayal of Women in CBC Programming--Policy Statement.)

This policy was approved by the CBC's Board of Directors and has been in effect since December 10, 1979. It has been distributed to all Corporation staff, including contract personnel where appropriate.

We believe that this program policy constitutes a genuine frame of reference for actions designed to eliminate stereotyped images of women.

However, the mere enunciation of a policy does not automatically ensure its immediate application.

To ensure implementation of this policy, the Corporation has prepared language guidelines. (See Addendum 3. Language Guidelines--Portrayal of Women in CBC Programs.) They contain nine points in English and five in French. These guidelines were distributed to all staff in April-May 1980 and were accompanied by an explanatory memo signed by the Assistant General Manager of each division. The memorandum reminded all employees of the importance of language, of the need to treat men and women equally, to use terms that include men and women, to use neutral-sounding words to describe occupations and professions, and so on. While the language guidelines have not received unanimous approval either inside or outside the

112

Corporation, it is clearly understood that they express the spirit of the CBC's commitment to the portrayal of women in its programs and that they are to be respected.

As a further means of implementing the program policy, two social affairs reporters in television news have been appointed, one at Toronto and the other at Montréal. Their duties are to ensure comprehensive coverage of events of national importance that are of particular interest to women. While this does not bar their male colleagues from also covering events in this field, the appointment of these two journalists is an indication of our determination to give a larger place to women on the national scene.

It was essential, if a program policy was to be effectively implemented, that production staff be thoroughly sensitized to the issue. A series of twelve seminars was held in the English Division of the Corporation in the winter of 1980. An assessment of this first venture indicated that it was necessary to redesign the format and content. A new series of seminars is therefore in preparation, this time using the expertise of the training and development office of the French Division. This new series of seminars is scheduled to begin in the fall of 1981, and if successful will be made available in both French and English.

Still with respect to programming, we committed ourselves to establishing a process for evaluating programs in order to monitor the implementation and effectiveness of these objectives. The CBC has a number of monitoring systems, but none which enables us to evaluate fully our portrayal of women. However, in order to provide the foundation for some future comparative evaluation of our progress, we have commissioned a substantial research project based on a study of three weeks of programming (January and

February 1981) on the English and French networks. In total, some 150 hours of programming are being studied. This is prime time programming (from 7 p.m. to 11:30 p.m.), excluding feature films and hockey games.

The study is designed to give us a detailed picture of the portrayal of women in a sizeable sample of our programs (content analysis), and to tell us how this portrayal is perceived by three separate groups--one drawn from the general public, one from CBC production personnel, and one from women with a feminist point of view.

The study is being conducted by a Toronto firm, PEAC, in cooperation with a professor from the University of Montréal. The firm is using new research equipment, adapted to our needs, which will also be used to inform our personnel of the results of the study. The content analysis is almost completed; audience research should begin in June and we should have the results in July. Although it does not in itself constitute a monitoring system, this study will, on the one hand, enable us to pinpoint the areas requiring attention and, on the other hand, serve as a solid starting point for further studies of its kind.

It should be noted that even though this study deals only with television, CBC programming policies apply to both radio and television. Moreover, these policies would also apply if the CBC were to create new networks (Télé-2 and CBC-2), since, in the application made to the CRTC, it is specified that these new networks are to give priority to groups who feel that they are under-served by the original networks. Women are clearly one of these groups.

b. Advertising: With respect to commercials, the CBC committed itself to carrying out a study of the publicity material it broadcasts. This study was completed during the winter of 1981. The research was designed to explain what is meant by stereotyping and to identify its manifestations.

Included with the study is a cassette of some 50 commercials. We have begun to use it to sensitize our personnel to the presence of stereotypes in commercials.

Even before this consciousness-raising initiative was taken, the CBC's commercial acceptance policy was changed. The section on Good Taste (Addendum 4) now reads:

> Commercials that have the effect of demanding audience attention by the use of the shock value of double entendre, or that exploit sex or nudity to achieve this same purpose, go against the normal standards of good or acceptable taste.

and:

> Also individuals or groups must not because of age, occupation, creed or sex be disparaged or unfairly represented. The Corporation is sensitive to sex-role stereotyping in broadcast advertising, and believes advertisers should endeavour to represent both sexes fairly in all types of roles.

As has always been the case, the (policy) on unacceptable advertising lists feminine hygiene products among the products for which the CBC does not accept advertising. The Corporation has also given its support in principle to the guidelines issued by the advertising industry.

c. Complaints: One of the difficult areas of our activity in connection with the portrayal of women is the handling of complaints. The Corporation has committed itself several times in the past to remaining open and receptive to comments from listeners and viewers, and the commitment applies also to the portrayal of women. However, the networks are large and the stations numerous, and it is difficult to be everywhere at once. We therefore offer the following suggestions:

For local or regional programs

Write or telephone to the producer of the program. This is the person who is really responsible for the program, and it is the producer's responsibility to make sure that researchers and announcers respect the policies. If the producer's name is not known, the complaint should be addressed to the head of audience relations or to the station manager.

For network programs

Here, too, it is important to contact the producer, or appeal to the person in charge of community relations in Montréal and Toronto.

In every instance, it is important to note the name of the program, the time and date of broadcast and any other useful information such as: city where broadcast is heard, announcer, etc.

If the complaint is put in writing, it is always advisable to send a copy to: Coordinator, Portrayal of Women, Canadian Broadcasting Corporation, P.O. Box 8478, 1500 Bronson Avenue, Ottawa, Ontario K1G 3J5.

d. Input: The activities of the Coordinator's office are not limited to the items described above. Since this position was created in May 1979, we have constantly approached various members of our staff to make sure that events of special interest to women receive the necessary attention. In addition, we have broadened our contacts with representatives of women's groups to inform them of our commitments and our policies. Since September 1980, there have been no fewer than twenty informal meetings of this kind.

iii. Equal Opportunity in the CBC

In May of 1974, the President of the CBC formed a six-member Task Force to study the situation and status of women employees within the Corporation. After an exhaustive survey and analysis, the group recommended that the CBC undertake a long-term, comprehensive equal opportunity program to be led by an office of equal opportunity which would be established immediately.

Accordingly, the Office of Equal Opportunity (OEO) was set up in August 1975. Structurally, the Office was placed within the Human Resources organization, with its head office personnel reporting directly to the Vice-President, Human Resources and its divisional officers reporting to their respective HR directors.

Of the more than 50 specific recommendations put forward by the Task Force, some 28 have now been fully implemented and the majority of the remainder are in the process of being implemented. (See Addendum 5. CBC Task Force on the Status of Women: Recommendations and Implementation, January 1981.)

In addition to ensuring the implementation of these specific recommendations, which basically resulted in the elimination of systemic discrimination in the CBC and the elaboration of the Corporation's equal opportunity/affirmative action policy for women, (Addendum 6), the Office of Equal Opportunity developed two major attitude awareness projects. The first had as its target audience the women of the CBC; the second, the managers and decision makers of the Corporation. The career awareness seminars for women were seen as a necessary first step toward the development and the better utilization of the CBC's female staff. A majority of women in the target group have been offered this 3-day seminar and results have been measurably encouraging.

The awareness project for managers has been comprised of an on-going series of briefings and consultations as well as more formal attitude awareness seminars designed to further understanding and appreciation of the problems facing CBC women today and to ensure the active involvement of all line managers in the equal opportunity efforts.

The major accomplishments of the OEO to date have been the elimination of systemic discrimination; the acceptance of an affirmative action plan with special measures for qualified women being embraced by the senior management; the incorporation of affirmative action goals into the Executive Vice-President's operating objectives and the endorsement of this principle by the heads of all units of the Corporation and a dramatic change in the CBC climate since the 1974 Task Force report. Tangible results are also evident though progress, as in all social change, is slow.

In 1980 the OEO received renewed support from the Board of Directors for its affirmative action program and the President reinforced his personal commitment in a communication to his senior management group. With achievement of the affirmative action objectives remaining such a high corporate priority and with the supportive internal climate, it is now anticipated that the rate of change will begin to increase in the coming months.

iv. Stereotypes Generally

As a result of the discussion which took place during the development of our program policy on portrayal of women in CBC programs, the CBC Board of Directors also requested the development of a broader program policy covering the whole question of stereotypes in our programming. This policy was formally proclaimed in October 1980 and is annexed as Addendum 7.

This document is a summary of our activities in the matter of the portrayal of women and equal opportunity; it is in no way exhaustive. However, we believe that it is a fair reflection of the extent of the efforts that have been made and we hope that the members of the Task Force will be reassured as to the value of our commitments and the responsible approach which we bring to our task.

Addendum 1. Excerpts from the Transcripts of the 1978 CRTC Hearings

CBC President A.W. Johnson: Another element of this old question of reflecting the reality of contemporary society is the proper portrayal of women. Women in our programming are very important, very difficult, and a very social and socially moving requirement.

I was struck, as I am sure all of you were, by the excellent interventions by a number of women's organizations. Again, we agree that the full contribution of women in contemporary society must be reflected on our programs and not some stereotype from the past. I don't accept any proposition that the CBC lacks the will to achieve this goal, nor that we have failed to show leadership, but it is incontestable that Canadian society has a long way to go and that we must listen to the constructive advice which women's groups are offering and can offer.

Let me be more specific. I and my senior colleagues propose to begin discussions with representatives of the major women's groups (and) organizations in the country. I would propose to have a two-day seminar as soon as we can arrange that and we will be talking about the questions and the issues which were raised before you. ...

Secondly, on the question of commercials: I think that the broadcasting industry has to attack this question along with the advertisers, and I would like to propose to you ... that the CRTC chair a group made up of the representatives of the broadcasters, representatives of women's organizations across the country, (and) representatives of the advertising industry, in an effort to come to grips with the question which really has been talked about a great deal, but about (which) not much action has been taken.

What is involved in all of these questions ... concerning the reflection of contemporary society, is, it seems to me, a matter of understanding and recognition in our present programming. It is not a matter of more money. We need more money for certain things, but it's a matter of contributing to that sense of worth, that sense of dignity, that sense of place which emerges for any group, for all of us when we are recognized as being an important and a contributing part of the society.

Addendum 2. Portrayal of Women in CBC Programming--Policy Statement

The CBC accepts as part of its mandate the need to reflect in its programming the role of women in Canadian society and to examine its social and political consequences. The CBC believes that its programming should also contribute to the understanding of issues affecting women.

In applying this policy, CBC programming should:

1. avoid the use of demeaning sexual stereotypes and sexist language;

2. reflect women and their interests in the reporting and discussion of current events;

3. recognize the full participation of women in Canadian society;

4. seek women's opinions on the full range of public issues.

Addendum 3. Language Guidelines--Portrayal of Women in CBC Programs

Words can be the symbols of deeply rooted cultural assumptions. The way language is now used tends to relegate women to secondary status in our society. Rules of correct grammatical usage, like rules of social conduct, are not immutable and may change to reflect changing social mores. The following guidelines are not lists of proscribed words. They provide examples which can broaden the use of language while avoiding sexist bias. The guidelines should be applied with awareness and judgment.

1. Include all people in general references by substituting neutral words and phrases for "man-words."

Examples:

INSTEAD OF	SUBSTITUTE
man-made	artificial, synthetic
man's achievements	human achievements
mankind	humanity, the human race, people
career women	name the profession

2. Avoid assuming that everyone in a group is male--or female.

Examples:

"the men in the cabinet"
"the boys in the caucus"
"the girls in the hairdressing shop"
"the doctor, he"
"the nurse, she"
(examples taken off-air)

3. Refer to women and men equally and make references consistent.

Examples:

NOT	RATHER
Mr. Sam Jones and Mary Smith	Sam Jones and Mary Smith, or Mr. Sam Jones and appropriate title Mary Smith

4. Avoid using "man" or "woman" as suffix or prefix in job titles.

Examples:

NOT	RATHER
mail boy	courier, messenger
policewoman or man	police officer
steward, stewardess	flight attendant

5. Use parallel language when referring to people by sex.

Examples:

NOT	RATHER
man and wife	husband and wife
ladies and men	women and men, ladies and gentlemen, girls and boys
men's teams and girls' teams	men's teams and women's teams

6. Avoid offensive or patronizing language, tokenism.

Examples:

NOT	RATHER
the little lady, better half	wife, spouse
libber, women's lib	feminist, women's movement

7. Grant equal respect to women and men. Do not describe men by professional position and women by physical attributes.

Examples:

NOT	RATHER
Sam Jones is a successful lawyer and his wife is a charming blonde.	Find out what his wife-- name--is involved in.

8. Use generic titles or descriptions for both women and men.

Examples:

NOT	RATHER
woman manager	manager
male secretary	secretary

9. Base communication on qualities that are pertinent to the story. Avoid words and visuals which emphasize physical features and clothes unless they are germane, and unless comparable terms would be used regardless of the subject's sex. Use the same standards for men and women in deciding whether to mention marital and family situations. In other words, write and edit with a

sense of equality, appropriateness and dignity for both
sexes.

Addendum 4. CBC Commercial Acceptance Policy Directive, 12 June 1980: CBC Standards of Good Taste

It is impossible to define good taste except in the most
general terms. There is no single standard. The truth
of this statement in a country as big as Canada with its
many regional dissimilarities is self-evident. It is a
basic requirement of Commercial Acceptance to ensure
that all commercial material intended for use on CBC
facilities meets the Corporation's interpretation of
good or acceptable taste in word, tone and scene.

Nothing can be judged to be in good or bad taste except
in relation to the context in which it appears. The
same phrase or visual presentation that legitimately
contributes to a drama may be totally inappropriate
when used in a commercial message. The viewer can
exercise a choice in program viewing but not in
commercial viewing.

Broadcasting is a guest in the home. All broadcast
advertising on CBC facilities must therefore meet the
Corporation's standards as to its suitability for
introduction into the intimacy of the home, in mixed
company, and in family or social groups. Commercials
that have the effect of demanding audience attention
by the use of the shock value of double entendre, or
that exploit sex or nudity to achieve this same purpose,
go against the normal standards of good or acceptable
taste.

The various characteristics of racial or ethnic
backgrounds or religious convictions must be treated
with dignity and decency, as must such things as
physical, mental, or speech imperfections. They must
not be held up as subjects of ridicule. Also individuals

or groups must not because of age, occupation, creed or sex be disparaged or unfairly represented. The Corporation is sensitive to sex-role stereotyping in broadcast advertising, and believes advertisers should endeavour to represent both sexes fairly in all types of roles.

Commercial appeals should be built upon frameworks within the moral, ethical, and legal standards of current society. Commercial approaches should not encourage or depict as being desirable any activity that is contrary to widely held standards of correct behaviour, especially in messages that might influence children. Messages that show blatant disregard for ecology or for the safety and rights of others are unacceptable.

Even the correct use of language properly belongs in this area of good taste. Although broadcast advertising uses a colloquial as opposed to a literary style of language, slang, dialect, or incorrect syntax should be accepted only when they are necessary, as in portraying particular character types. They should not be accepted in a form that by implication holds up such usage as a model of acceptable speech.

Commercial messages must be produced in such a way as to avoid an impression of excessive loudness and be presented at a pace that can be comfortably followed. (A maximum of 150 words per minute is a standard that is frequently followed.)

The final decision as to the acceptability of any commercial material relating to the Corporation's standards of good taste rests with the Commercial Acceptance Department, and any problems regarding its interpretation should be directed to the Commercial Acceptance Policy office, Head Office.

Addendum 5. CBC Task Force on the Status of Women:
Recommendations and Implementation, January 1981

RECOMMENDATION

1. Overall policy

    Develop and communicate throughout the
    Corporation an equal opportunity policy with
    detailed guidelines for its implementation.
    - Implemented.

2. Job access--employment

    Revise all recruitment materials to eliminate sex
    stereotyping. -Implemented.

3. Job access--employment

    Communicate new equal opportunity policy to all
    major sources of outside candidates for
    employment. -Implemented.

4. Job access--employment

    Ensure that all external employment advertising
    invites both men and women applicants.
    -Implemented.

5. Job access--employment

    Work with unions to remove--where practical--sex
    from position titles. -Implemented.

6. Job access--employment

    Revise application forms to remove questions on
    sex and marital status, and encourage use of
    initials rather than first names. -Implemented.

7. Job access--employment

Redesign notice of vacancy form to include invitation to both men and women applicants. -Implemented.

8. Job access--employment

Develop new interview guidelines and circulate to all employment personnel and supervisors. -Implemented.

9. Job access--employment

Post all jobs up to and including MS V. -Implemented.

10. Job access--employment

Have human resources planning personnel, working with the Office of Equal Opportunity, develop an inventory of women, to be consulted by decision makers. -In discussion.

11. Job access--employment

Establish selection boards for all vacancies from above lowest entry level up to and including MS V. -Implemented.

12. Job access--training

Ensure that awareness sessions are built into the supervisory training program that is being developed in 1975/76. -On going.

13. Job access--training

Conduct pilot awareness sessions outside supervisory training, using professional resources, extend these sessions across the CBC if they are successful. -On going.

14. Overall action program--affirmative action

    Develop and implement affirmative action programs to increase the proportion of women in management and other key jobs, and to break down segregation by sex in positions at lower levels. -On going.

15. Overall action program--affirmative action

    Carry out the action programs on a decentralized basis, working with senior managers. -On going.

16. Overall action program--monitoring

    Monitor, through the Office of Equal Opportunity, progress both in the Corporation as a whole and in individual locations. -On going.

17. Overall action program--reports

    Present, through the Office of Equal Opportunity, regular reports to management on the progress--or lack of progress--in the matter of job access in the Corporation as a whole and in individual locations, and issue an annual report to all employees. -On going.

18. Secretaries

    Establish an action program that gives special encouragement to qualified secretaries to advance into administration and production. -In process.

19. Secretaries

Undertake, as a first step, a project in an English Services region outside Toronto to design and implement new advancement paths. -In process.

20. Secretaries

Abolish rug ranking, and institute instead a job evaluation plan for stenographers and secretaries. -In process.

21. Secretaries

Use the project team approach for designing and implementing the plan, working at the same English Services locations as for the advancement project. -In process.

22. Secretaries

Develop detailed job descriptions for secretaries, starting with the English Services pilot project. -In process.

23. Secretaries

Seek to increase the number of men engaged in secretarial functions. -In discussion.

24. Secretaries

Ensure that a session on boss-secretary relationships is incorporated in supervisory training. -In discussion.

25. Compensation--salaries

   Develop and distribute to all employees an overall
   equal pay policy and guidelines for its
   administration. -In discussion.

26. Compensation--salaries

   Request, following the issuance of that policy, that
   all supervisors review the salaries of men and
   women in identical position categories, to
   determine whether differences are justified.
   -In discussion.

27. Compensation--salaries

   Review annually all entry salaries and position-
   by-position comparisons, and follow up apparent
   anomalies with the supervisors concerned.
   -In process.

28. Compensation--salaries

   Incorporate materials on unconscious
   discrimination in salary administration into general
   supervisory training. -In discussion.

29. Compensation--salaries

   Conduct a separate examination of the pay of
   contract personnel. -In discussion.

30. Compensation--benefits

   Equalize coverage under the Group Life Plan,
   within 9 months. -Implemented.

31. Compensation--benefits

    Investigate the possibility of a later revision of the
    plan to introduce optional coverage.
    -Implemented.

32. Compensation--benefits

    Equalize survivor benefits. -Implemented.

33. Compensation--benefits

    Investigate the possibility of broadening the
    definition of dependents to that used in the Income
    Tax Act, with the understanding that only one
    adult could be named as a dependent, along with
    dependent children as presently defined.
    -In discussion.

34. Compensation--benefits

    Implement immediately the Corporate Personnel
    revision of the definition of "dependents" in the
    Northern Allowance policy. -Implemented.

35. Compensation--benefits

    Change all references from "wife" to "spouse" in
    both policy and forms that describe Transfer and
    Removal Allowances. -Implemented.

36. Responsibilities of parenthood--maternity and
    paternity leave

    Establish, for employees with 1 year of service or
    more a separate paid paternity leave, to be
    included in an overall birth policy. -Implemented.

37. Responsibilities of parenthood--maternity and paternity leave

    Set the leave entitlement at 3 days.
    -Implemented.

38. Responsibilities of parenthood--maternity and paternity leave

    Pay for women, with a minimum of 1 year's service, full salary and the Corporation's share of benefit costs during maternity leave for a period of up to 15 weeks, to be taken at her discretion, provided she signifies her intention to return.
    -Partially implemented. -In discussion.

39. Responsibilities of parenthood--maternity and paternity leave

    Guarantee the new mother the identical position upon her return. -In discussion.

40. Responsibilities of parenthood--child care

    Undertake to provide assistance to employees in obtaining improved child care facilities.
    -Implemented.

41. Responsibilities of parenthood--child care

    Undertake, as a first step, a feasibility study in Montréal to determine what form the assistance should take. -Implemented.

42. Overall action program--Office of Equal Opportunity

    Undertake a long-term equal opportunity program, which would phase in the recommended changes over a period of 3 to 4 years. -Implemented.

43. Overall action program—Office of Equal Opportunity

Create an Office of Equal Opportunity (OEO) and direct it to give top priority to implementing the program to ensure equal opportunity for women in the CBC. -Implemented.

44. Overall action program—Office of Equal Opportunity

Establish the following positions within the OEO, reporting to the senior human resources manager.

- At the corporate level, a Director reporting to the Vice-President, Human Resources, and supported by two coordinators and a research analyst. -Implemented.

- In each division, an equal opportunity officer who reports to the Director, Human Resources. -Implemented.

- In each region, an equal opportunity representative, who may be full- or part-time, and who reports to the senior personnel officer. -Not to be implemented.

45. Overall action program—Office of Equal Opportunity

Staff the OEO using the selection board process. -Implemented.

46. Overall action program—other mechanisms

Create equal opportunity committees at each of the corporate, divisional, and regional levels. -Not to be implemented.

47. Overall action program--other mechanisms

   Report annually to the CBC's Board of Directors on
   progress in the equal opportunity program.
   -Implemented.

48. Overall action program--other mechanisms

   Include pressing equal opportunity items on the
   agendas of regular senior management meetings.
   -Implemented.

49. Overall action program--other mechanisms

   Set annual equal opportunity objectives down to
   the level of large locations. -On going.

Addendum 6. Equal Opportunity of Employment Policy

The report of the Task Force on the Status of Women in
the CBC, tabled in May 1975, revealed certain
inequities in employment and career opportunities for
female employees, and convinced the Corporation of
the desirability to reaffirm its general policy of equal
opportunity for all categories of employees.

It is the policy of the CBC as an employer to ensure
that employment, training and development, and other
career opportunities are available to everyone,
regardless of such considerations as race, national or
ethnic origin, religion, age, sex or sexual orientation, or
marital status.

Hiring and promotion procedures must reflect this
policy. Where past practices or role stereotyping have
resulted in the exclusion of valuable human resources or
the underutilization of any employee, group or groups
of employees, the Corporation will introduce positive
corrective measures.

A temporary Office of Equal Opportunity has been created to provide guidance on the appropriate actions and corrective measures deemed necessary to ensure fair treatment and equality of opportunities for all employees.

Human Resources Directors and Managers are responsible, at all times, for ensuring that this policy is implemented and for enlisting the cooperation of all managers.

Addendum 7. Stereotypes in CBC Programming--Policy

1. "Stereotype" may be defined as: "a fixed or conventional notion or conception, as of a person, group, idea, etc., held by a number of people, and allowing for no individuality, critical judgment, etc." (Webster's New World Dictionary, 1974)

2. Stereotypes are generalizations, drawn from perceptions that certain qualities and characteristics are commonly shared by certain groupings in society, reflecting race, national, regional or ethnic origin, religion, age, sex, marital status, physical attributes or occupation. Ill-advised use of stereotypes tends to reinforce prejudices, and constitutes an assault on the dignity of the individual.

3. Those responsible for program content should be alert to the cumulative power of the electronic media to shape tastes and to contribute to the definition of individual and social ideals, and, therefore, should refrain from indiscriminate portrayal of detrimental stereotypes. Common sense, good judgment, and good taste should be part of the basic discipline of all production and on-air broadcasters, who should not only present persons as individuals, but also challenge stereotypes when these may be introduced uncritically by other participants.

4. Stereotyping in CBC programming is acceptable only when it is essential to the realisation of a program's purpose. The use of stereotype characters in CBC presentations may arise only from requirement of the plot, such as in drama, comedies, etc.

APPENDIX 5

CANADIAN ASSOCIATION OF BROADCASTERS

A. Canadian Association of Broadcasters Code of Ethics

Clause 1. General Programming

Recognizing the varied tastes of the public, it shall be the responsibility of the broadcasting industry to so programme its various stations that as far as possible, all groups of listeners and viewers shall have from these, some part of the programming devoted to their special likes and desires.

Clause 2. Children's Programmes

Recognizing that programmes designed specifically for children reach impressionable minds and influence social attitudes and aptitudes, it shall be the responsibility of member stations to provide the closest possible supervision in the selection and control of material, characterization and plot. Nothing in the foregoing shall mean that the vigour and vitality common to children's imaginations and love of adventure should be removed. It does mean that programmes should be based upon sound social concepts and presented with a superior degree of craftsmanship; that these programmes should reflect the moral and ethical standards of contemporary Canadian society and encourage pro-social behaviour and attitudes. The member station should encourage parents to select from the richness of broadcasting fare, the best programmes to be brought to the attention of their children.

Clause 3. Community Activities

It shall be the responsiblity of each member station to serve to the utmost of its ability the interests of its

138

particular community and to identify itself actively
with worthwhile community activities.

Clause 4. Education

While recognizing that all programmes possess, by their
very nature, some educational value, member stations
will do all in their power to make specific educational
efforts as useful and entertaining as possible. To that
end, they will continue to use their time and facilities
and to cooperate with appropriate educational groups in
an attempt to augment the educational and cultural
influences of school, institutions of higher learning, the
home and other institutions devoted to education and
culture. When practical, advantage should be taken of
opportunities to consult such institutions on what
suitable material is available and how it may best be
presented. Where practical, factual material for public
enlightenment should be included by stations, networks,
advertisers and their agencies.

Clause 5. News

It shall be the responsibility of member stations to
ensure that news shall be presented with accuracy and
without bias. The member station shall satisfy itself
that the arrangements made for obtaining news ensure
this result. It shall also ensure that news broadcasts
are not editorial. News shall not be selected for the
purpose of furthering or hindering either side of any
controversial public issue, nor shall it be coloured by
the beliefs or opinions or desires of the station
management, the editor or others engaged in its
preparation or delivery. The fundamental purpose of
news dissemination in a democracy is to enable people
to know what is happening and to understand events so
that they may form their own conclusions.

Therefore, nothing in the foregoing shall be understood as preventing news broadcasters from analyzing and elucidating news so long as such analysis or comment is clearly labelled as such and kept distinct from regular news presentations. Member stations will, insofar as practical, endeavour to provide editorial opinion which shall be clearly labelled as such and kept entirely distinct from regular broadcasts of news, or analysis and opinion.

It is recognized that the full, fair and proper presentation of news, opinion, comment, and editorial is the prime and fundamental responsibility of the broadcast publisher.

Clause 6. Controversial Public Issues

Recognizing in a democracy the necessity of presenting all sides of a public issue, it shall be the responsibility of member stations to treat fairly, all subjects of a controversial nature. Time shall be allotted with due regard to all the other elements of balanced programme schedules, and to the degree of public interest in the questions presented. Recognizing that healthy controversy is essential to the maintenance of democratic institutions, the broadcast publisher will endeavour to encourage presentation of news and opinion on any controversy which contains an element of the public interest.

Clause 7. Advertising

Recognizing the service that commercial sponsors render to listeners and viewers in making known to them the goods and services available in their communities, and realizing that the story of such goods and services goes into the intimacy of the home, it shall be the responsibility of member stations and their sales representatives to work with advertisers and agencies in improving the technique of telling the advertising story so that these shall be in good taste, shall be simple, truthful and believable, and shall not offend what is generally accepted as the prevailing standard of good taste.

Advertising is to be made most effective not only by the use of an appropriate selling message but by earning the most favourable reaction of the public to the sponsor by providing the best possible programming. Nothing in the foregoing shall prevent the dramatization of the use, value, or attractiveness of products and services. While appropriate legislation protects the public from false and exaggerated claims for drugs, proprietaries and foods, it shall be the responsibility of member stations and sales representatives to work with the advertisers of these products, and the advertising agencies, to ensure that their value and use are told in words that are not offensive. Recognizing also that advertising appeals or commentaries by any advertiser, that cast reflection upon the operations of a competitor or other industry or business, are destructive of public confidence, it shall be the responsibility of member stations, so far as it lies within their power, to prevent such advertising appeals or commentaries being broadcast by their stations.

Broadcasters subscribing to the Code of Ethics and Clause 7, approve adherence to the complementary Canadian Code of Advertising Standards, published by the Canadian Advertising Advisory Board; the Broadcast Code of Advertising to Children, published by the Canadian Association of Broadcasters; and to the Code of Consumer Advertising Practices for Non-Prescription Medicines, as published by the Canadian Advertising Advisory Board, and endorsed by the Board of the Canadian Association of Broadcasters.

Clause 8. Treatment of Religious Programmes

The broadcaster should endeavour to make available to the community adequate opportunity for presentation of religious messages, and should also endeavour to assist in all ways open to him or her the furtherance of religious activities in the community. Recognizing the purpose of the religious broadcast to be that of promoting the spiritual harmony and understanding of mankind and that of administering broadly to the varied religious needs of the community, it shall be the responsibility of each member station to ensure that its religious broadcasts, which reach men of all creeds and races simultaneously, shall not be used to convey attacks upon another race or religion.

Clause 9. Employees

Each member station shall endeavour to secure the highest possible type of employees and people who are qualified for, and suitable to, the duties for which each is hired. Every attempt shall be made to make service in the broadcasting industry an attractive and permanent career, permitting employees to contribute through their manner of living and personal attainments to the station's prestige in the community. Each employee shall receive, in addition to minimum guarantees provided by applicable legislation, fair remuneration and treatment in accordance with the standards prevailing in the particular community at any time. The general intent of this section is the realization that any industry is most often judged by the type of employees it attracts; the manner in which they conduct themselves and are able to live; and their opinion of the industry for which they work. Recognizing this as a valuable asset, the broadcaster will do everything possible to maintain and further the best type of staff relations.

Clause 10. Adherence

a. All future broadcasting codes which have been endorsed by the Board of Directors and ratified by the membership who subscribe to the Code, at a duly called annual meeting of the Association, shall be incorporated into the Code of Ethics.

b. Upon adoption of this Code of Ethics by the Association, any member broadcasting station shall be granted appropriate recognition and symbol. It may then make announcement periodically of the fact it is in possession of such certification and be entitled to make appropriate aural and visual use of the Code symbol.

Clause 11. Composition of the Committee

There shall be a Code of Ethics Committee of five persons, three of whom shall be appointed by the Board of Directors, and two elected by the annual meeting of the Association, for a period not to exceed five years, and appointments may be renewed. Any vacancy in the Committee may be filled for the unexpired term by the Board of Directors. Any vacancy or absence shall not impair the powers of the remaining members of the Code of Ethics Committee to act, provided however that a quorum of it shall be considered as not less than three persons and such a quorum shall be present before the Code of Ethics Committee is empowered to transact business.

B. **Sex-Role Stereotyping Report of the Canadian Association of Broadcasters**

i. Background to Resolution 13

During the 1981 Annual General Meeting of the Canadian Association of Broadcasters, convened in

Québec City, the delegates heard, discussed, and passed Resolution Number 13 dealing with the matter of sex-role stereotyping. (The resolution is included as Addendum 2.)

This resolution called for the immediate establishment of a special committee "whose responsibilities will be to examine and to recommend ways and means whereby the radio and television members of the Association can, to the best of their abilities, ensure":

- that the programming produced by or for member stations and networks "reflect a sensitivity to the problems related to sex-role stereotyping";

- that "the language used in programming should be of an inclusive nature, avoiding wherever possible expressions which relate only to one gender"; and

- that "programming should reflect the intellectual and emotional equality of both sexes."

The resolution evolved as a consequence of the Association's involvement in the proceedings of the Canadian Radio-television and Telecommunications Commission's Task Force on Sex-Role Stereotyping in the Broadcast Media, which was formed in September 1979; and a meeting between the CAB Board of Directors' Executive Committee and representatives of the CRTC Task Force, composed of members of the various media, the advertising industry and public representatives, including representatives of recognized feminist organizations.

The Task Force determined that its responsibility was to investigate the best method of ensuring that sex-role stereotyping was recognized and to develop some mechanism to correct the problem. Public sector Task Force members developed a consensus of concerns based on research studies from the last ten years, which showed that some elements of advertising and programming are considered insulting to women.

The early work of the Commission's Task Force centered on the issue of sex-role stereotyping in advertising messages in the broadcast media. This resulted in initiatives undertaken by the advertising industry including representatives from the Canadian Association of Broadcasters, which led to the formation of an awareness program primarily developed for professional practitioners of advertising, known as "Women Say the Darndest Things." The central theme of the short film and its accompanying literature is the sensitization of people engaged in the advertising process--in particular, the creative aspect--to the problems in perception of sex-role stereotyping, especially regarding the portrayal of women in commercials. Although the film entitled "Women Say the Darndest Things" is directed mainly towards advertisers, the Canadian Association of Broadcasters has underwritten a substantial portion of its production cost.

At a later stage in the proceedings of the CRTC Task Force, the focus shifted to the aspect of the portrayal of women in broadcast programming. At this stage in the evolution of the dialogue, the CAB undertook its own initiatives on behalf of private broadcasters.

ii. The CAB Resolution

The resolution identifies the problem of sex-role stereotyping, and the CAB acknowledges "that stereotypic images of men, women, boys and girls are perpetuated and reinforced, and to some extent even seemingly legitimized, by the mass dissemination of these images." It continues, stating that, "such stereotypic images constitute a limiting or a narrowing of society's perception of men and of women and their roles" and that such images "can and do cause negative and countervailing influences." These are the influences which the broadcaster must be conscious of and avoid. The resolution preamble was followed by a broad and general statement of essential CAB beliefs:

- that "the Association sustains the opinion that the best and most effective regulation is voluntary self-regulation";

- that the CAB "reasserts its respect for the creative freedoms expressed in the production of programs and advertising messages";

- that the CAB "continues its belief in the right of free expression of opinions and ideas"; and lastly,

- that the CAB "holds to the view that goods and services lawfully available to the Canadian public should be permitted to be advertised in broadcasting without undue restraint selectively applied to the media."

Incorporated within that statement of beliefs was a companion declaration that the CAB "acknowledges that sex-role stereotyping, while not a recent social phenomenon, constitutes a contemporary problem."

The CAB, through its members, will allow the broadcast media to adapt to this new awareness and assist in finding ways to more accurately represent the role of women in contemporary society.

iii. The Issue Re-examined from the Broadcasters' Perspective

No other element of Canadian media is as regulated as is broadcasting; consequently, broadcasters bear a particular vulnerability in the context of emerging social issues such as sex-role stereotyping. The publicity attached to the deliberations of the CRTC's Task Force has, in the minds of some, attached an undue responsibility for an involvement in the issue of stereotyping by broadcasters. With this perception has developed, again largely because of the publicity, a sense of belief that stereotyping per se is a negative proposition.

While everyone agrees that no single medium can be held more accountable than another for negative stereotyping, there is no question that broadcasting has greater mass appeal and therefore greater vulnerability, especially given its regulatory environment. Broadcasters consequently must bear both an artificial and disproportionate burden of responsibility--both for the existence of negative stereotyping and, as well, for the perception of a capacity for solutions. CAB is caught in the midst of a dilemma. Although it recognizes the reality of the problem and the fact that some elements of the broadcasting industry unwittingly do contribute to this social problem, it has limited opportunities to offer solutions. As an Association made up of voluntary membership by the majority of Canada's private broadcasters, the CAB cannot impose upon that membership rules and regulations which can be enforced in such a manner as to assure compliance. The task of this and all such committees therefore, is difficult, and dependent upon the level of consciousness of its members on this question. On the other hand, the Association can contribute to the resolution of the problem by developing programs designed to enhance the level of consciousness of its members.

iv. Existing Regulatory and Self-regulatory Pressures

Laws and Regulations

It is important to note that, in addition to the regulatory capacities of the Commission, the public interest in respect to sex-role stereotyping is served by federal and provincial statutes. Further to the traditional laws regarding libel, slander and defamation of character, are more recent enactments dealing with human rights.

The Canadian Human Rights Act of 1977 sets its purpose "to extend the present laws in Canada" to ensure that all persons may pursue their lives "without being hindered in or prevented from doing so by discriminatory practices based on race, national or ethnic origin, colour, religion, age, sex or marital status ... or by discriminatory employment practices."

Section 12 of the Human Rights Act states that: "It is a discriminatory practice to publish or display before the public or to cause to be published or displayed before the public any notice, sign, symbol, emblem or other representation that ... expresses or implies discrimination or an intention to discriminate, or... (that) incites or is calculated to incite others to discriminate."

The Act also established the Canadian Human Rights Commission, empowering it to set guidelines, receive complaints, investigate such complaints, and, where necessary, institute the impaneling of a human rights tribunal. The tribunal may order, when it finds cause in respect to a sustained complaint, "that such person cease such discriminatory practice and, in consultation with the Commission on the general purposes thereof, take measures, including adoption of a special program, plan or arrangement ... to prevent the same or a similar practice occurring in the future ... that such person compensate the victim, as the tribunal may consider proper ... (for) any expenses incurred by the victim as a result of the discriminatory practice." Failure to

comply with such an order could lead to a summary
conviction requiring fines "not exceeding fifty thousand
dollars."

Self-regulatory Pressures

In the Committee's opinion, broadcasting is constantly
regulated by two natural but seldom recognized forces:
the public (audiences), and the decision making
structure of the programming elements of broadcasting.

The member stations and networks of the Canadian
Association of Broadcasters operate services which are
entirely dependent upon the public response as
translated into the size of audience attained. In all
instances, station operators know quickly whether or
not their programming responds to the needs and
interests of their audiences. They know this through
personal contacts, telephone calls and letters. This
knowledge is frequently verified throughout the year by
way of audience surveys conducted regularly by two
national enterprises, the Bureau of Broadcast
Measurement and the A.C. Nielsen Company.

Broadcasters, in particular those privately operated
entities which are members of the Association, depend
entirely upon the revenues derived from the sale of air
time to advertisers for the scheduling of commercial
messages. That revenue, in turn, is directly related to
the audiences tuned to the program services offered by
the broadcasters.

A broadcasting operation which fails to respond
appropriately to the needs and interests of the public,
loses audience and, consequently, advertising
revenue--a double motive not to offend or antagonize
the public. That situation does not, of course,
eliminate the factor of human error or unplanned or
unwitting excess or exaggeration in aspects of

programming. But it does provide, at least to broadcasters, a sense of comfort in the realization that they simply cannot afford to alienate the public. Such strong self-regulatory pressures do exist despite the fact that they are often not well understood by the public.

The other functioning reality of broadcasting, which also serves as a form of control or balance against an improper or inappropriate use of the airwaves (beyond the scope of CRTC regulation or the requirements of the Broadcasting Act) is the multi-tiered decision making process which governs all aspects of program production. Except in the rarest of cases, no single individual is exclusively responsible for deciding what will be seen and/or heard on a broadcast service, including commercials. There are many stages and many levels of determination regarding content, enough to ensure in almost every single instance that only that which is acceptable goes to "air."

Broadcasters have an abiding respect for the creative forces employed within their services and as they relate to the provision of advertising messsages. Indeed it is this creative force which most contributes to the originality and popularity of broadcasting services. At the same time, broadcasters function within a volatile and spontaneous environment, frequently including the live presentation of events or information of broad, general interest on their schedules. They are therefore always concerned about influences, particularly those which may not represent the interests or opinions of the general public, which may be brought to bear upon these aspects of creativity and spontaneity in such a way as to limit or minimize their effective and valued contributions.

v. Conclusions and Recommendations

Having fully considered all factors known and made available, the CAB Committee examined ways and means whereby broadcasters could contribute to the resolution of the problem of negative sex-role stereotyping as expressed at this point in time in our social evolution.

The Committee concluded that broadcasters, while bearing no unique responsibility for the creation of the problem of negative sex-role stereotyping in society, do share part of the general responsibility for its existence and consequently accept their share of responsibility for its elimination.

The Committee concluded that broadcasters, while recognizing they are regulated by the CRTC and are also subject to the laws regarding libel and slander, also recognize that there are provincial and federal statutes dealing with aspects of human relations.

Having regard to all of the above, the Committee recommended to the CAB Board of Directors that the Association, through the appropriate standing committees and, ultimately, through its member radio and television stations, (undertake) the following:

1. That the Code of Ethics of the Canadian Association of Broadcasters be amended as follows:

a. Following Clause 1, "General Programming," a new Clause 2 be added which reads:

"Clause 2. Human Rights

Recognizing that every person has a right to full and equal recognition and to enjoy certain fundamental rights and freedoms, broadcasters shall endeavour to

ensure, to the best of their ability, that their
programming contains no abusive or discriminatory
material or comment which is based on matters of race,
national or ethnic origin, colour, religion, age, sex,
marital status or physical or mental handicap."

b.   In respect to existing Clause 7, "Advertising," the
following words be inserted within the third paragraph
(second line, following "Canadian Advertising Advisory
Board"):

", and to its guidelines on sex-role stereotyping."

c.   Following Clause 8, "Treatment of Religious
Programmes," a new Clause 9 be added which reads:

"Clause 9. Sex-Role Stereotyping

Recognizing that stereotypic images can and do cause
negative and countervailing influences, it shall be the
responsibility of the broadcasters to reflect, to the best
of their ability, a conscious sensitivity of the problems
related to sex-role stereotyping, by refraining from
exploitation and by the reflection of the intellectual
and emotional equality of both sexes in programming."

2.   That the Association management develop and
prepare its own printed material dealing with sex-role
stereotyping and specifically with the aspect of
program production and, further, that both radio and
television members be encouraged to develop and
produce specific program material dealing with the
subject for part of an overall exchange of such
programs and as part of an awareness program amongst
the general membership and for the added benefit of
the public.

3.   That the Association embark immediately on an
information program designed to acquaint the public

with its participation in dealing with the issue of sex-role stereotyping.

4.   That the Association endorse and support the voluntary initiatives of the advertising industry in dealing with the issue of sex-role stereotyping, through the Canadian Advertising Advisory Board, and that, wherever practicable, member stations cooperate with locally organized or nationally conducted campaigns of the CAAB in this regard. In this respect, members of the Association may wish to make available to its audiences copies of whatever printed material is available on the subject, and television members, in particular, may be able to make use of the short film, partly funded by CAB, "Women Say The Darndest Things," which the CAAB may be able to make available.

5.   That broadcasters exercise their best efforts to use language of an inclusive nature in their programming, by avoiding whenever possible expressions which relate only to one gender.

Submitted to the CAB Board of Directors by the CAB Special Committee on Sex-Role Stereotyping.

Addendum 1. Additional Resolutions

The CAB Board of Directors received and accepted the report and recommendations of the CAB Special Committee on Sex-Role Stereotyping. The CAB Board of Directors also passed the following additional resolutions:

1.   That a workshop on sex-role stereotyping be held at the next CAB annual meeting.

2.   That the CAB implement recommendations 2 and 3 of the report by developing and implementing most of its program, as soon as possible, early in 1982.

3. That, as part of its program, the CAB shall examine the possibility of producing master tapes concerning the topic of sex-role stereotyping and to use its Program Exchange Service for the dissemination of this material.

4. That the CAB shall revive its Committee on Sex-Role Stereotyping to serve as the responsible body, to examine complaints received from the public, and to advise on the implementation of all CAB recommendations on sex-role stereotyping. This Committee or the CAB Education Committee will be responsible for the educative role proposed in the report.

Addendum 2. Resolution 13

Given that stereotypic images of men, women, boys and girls are perpetuated and reinforced, and to some extent even seemingly legitimized, by the mass dissemination of these images and

Given that such stereotypic images constitute a limiting or a narrowing of society's perception of men and of women and their roles, and that such stereotypic images can and do cause negative and countervailing influences,

be it resolved by the 1981 General Assembly of the Canadian Association of Broadcasters meeting in Québec City that:

1. The Association sustains the opinion that the best and most effective regulation is voluntary self-regulation, and that

2. The Association reasserts its respect for the creative freedoms expressed in the production of programs and advertising messages, and that

3. The Association continues its belief in the right of free expression of opinions and ideas, and that

4. The Association holds to the view that goods and services lawfully available to the Canadian public should be permitted to be advertised in broadcasting without undue restraint selectively applied to the media, but that

5. The Association also acknowledges that sex-role stereotyping, while not a recent social phenomenon, constitutes a contemporary problem, and therefore that

6. The Association, through its Board of Directors, will immediately constitute a committee whose responsibilities will be to examine and to recommend ways and means whereby the radio and television members of the Association can, to the best of their abilities, ensure:

   a. that programming reflect a conscious sensitivity of the problems related to sex-role stereotyping and

   b. that programming refrain from gratuitous exploitation of sex-role stereotyping and

   c. that the language used in programming should be of an inclusive nature, avoiding wherever possible expressions which relate only to one gender, and

   d. that programming should reflect the intellectual and emotional equality of both sexes.

   With respect to the issue as it relates to advertising messages, the Association recognizes the self-regulatory initiatives undertaken by the advertising industry and hereby pledges its support and endorsement of that voluntary action, and that

7. The Association expects the new committee to report to the Board and hence to the general membership, within three months of its constitution.

                                              -Carried.

Addendum 3. Sex Stereotyping in the Electronic Media: A Summary of Concerns

This section may be found in the main body of our report, Images of Women, Chapter 4, A Summary of Concerns.

APPENDIX 6

THE ADVERTISING INDUSTRY

A. Canadian Advertising Advisory Board--Task Force on Women and Advertising, 1977

i. Recommendations of the CAAB Task Force on Women and Advertising

Advertisers and Advertising Agencies

1. Our pilot study indicates that "liberated" messages can work well. When created with intelligence and good taste, they tend generally to outscore the "traditional" message. We recommend that national advertisers undertake more extensive research in this field.

2. Employment statistics change as rapidly as the world around us. Market pre-testing should be checked against present day life-style patterns. You may be missing out on the close to 50 per cent of women who work outside the home if your potential market sample is based on weekday afternoon interviews.

3. When women are included in advertisements, depict them as equals. It is regarded as a "put-down" when an advertiser uses women solely as decorative props rather than as responsible, prospective customers.

4. Personal care product advertising should be directed at a women's feeling for self-enhancement, rather than undermining her self-esteem or emphasizing the "man-trap" approach.

5. Humour in advertising calls for special skills. It may entertain and yet not sell the product, or it may demean and offend--and this applies to both

men and women--instead of creating customer goodwill. One test of a humorous advertisement is the question, "Would it offend me to be portrayed in that way?"

6. Frequently the basic problem with feminine portrayals on television is the cumulative impact. The task force recommends that advertisers with pools of commercials explore the opportunities inherent in directing messages to various segments in their target groups. Thus, some commercials could use non-homemakers with outside interests such as community affairs.

   A businesswoman could promote, for example, a convenience product, "because I'm a busy woman and my time with my family is important." Or depict other family members helping with or doing household tasks. Even when the mother is not working outside the home, many families share these responsibilities.

7. Depict people showing an intelligent interest in the benefits of household cleaning products and convenience foods--not hysterically impressed by them. Here the final execution is important. Even though the written words and described visual are on target, the talent direction and even the inflection of words can result in an exaggerated or annoying portrayal. The aim is to reflect priorities that coincide with the realities of today's world.

8. Purchasing decisions on some items--cars, appliances, liquor, and wine--are often made jointly by husband and wife. Sometimes they are purchased by a woman alone, with no male involvement, and this important market segment should not be ignored.

9.   When showing women working outside the home, expand the portrayals beyond the traditional job categories--nurses, secretaries, teachers, models, etc. Occupational choices have widened considerably in recent years and certainly some women operate at management levels.

10. Stereotypes are probably an inevitable component of mass communication. But some stereotypes of women invariably evoke, not a sense of identification but a sense of frustration, annoyance or outrage--"the witless housewife," "pretty but helpless," "the superservant". It is not a matter of avoiding stereotypes, rather of using good stereotypes.

11. Since many radio messages are read by the disc jockey, rather than pre-recorded, the number of advertisements with male announcers is over-whelmingly higher than female. An effort should be made to produce more pre-recorded radio advertisements using female announcers; and in TV, more women should be used as "voice-overs" and announcers rather than just product demonstrators.

Consumers

There seems to be a widespread feeling among consumers that complaints to companies about the quality of goods and services or the nature of advertising go unheeded. None of the business representatives on the task force shared this view. All could give examples of the impact of even a few letters to management. Naturally, not all advertisements--just as not all books, plays, or films--can be expected to please or appeal to everyone. But viewers, readers, and listeners who feel offended by an advertisement should let the medium and the company management know how they feel and not just talk to the neighbours.

By the same token, when consumers admire
advertisements created with imagination and good
taste, we suggest the time sometimes be taken to write
a note of praise. Individual voices can be influential
when heard in the right places.

Our media review indicates that many marketers are
aware of the changing nature of society, and their
messages reflect that awareness. Our hope is that this
report will help add to that number.

ii. Portrayals Checklist

As a general guide, the CAAB Task Force has
developed, from a variety of sources, a checklist of
positive and negative portrayals. We recommend its
use as a guide to positive portrayals of men and women.

Positive Portrayals	Negative Portrayals
	Sexual Stereotypes
both sexes intelligent, attractive, physically able	women silly, weak, over-emotional; double entendres especially about sex or women's bodies
products purchased for self-enhancement or self-enjoyment	use cosmetics mainly "to catch a man"; low intelligence, "dumb blond," can't handle a cheque book or operate a car properly; belittling language-- "weaker sex," etc.

Positive Portrayals	Negative Portrayals

Role Stereotypes

both sexes enjoy constructive, mentally stimulating activities	passive activity for girls in toy advertisements; boys engaged in creative, athletic, mind-enriching games
women and men in partnership supporting each other and sharing in family tasks	women's role essentially to cater to and coddle men and children--serve coffee, etc.
actualities of labour force data	mainly housewives, obsessed with cleanliness, naggers by nature, neurotic, condescending to other women; or as models and "adornments"
women also occupy professional and executive roles, both share in decision-making process	men make decisions, tell women what to do

Presence of Women in Advertising

Role portrayals feature women and men	low level of female voice-overs, authority figures; low presence of women when buying big-ticket items; different portrayal of men vs. women as product representatives

161

Positive Portrayals	Negative Portrayals
Special Problems	
often a matter of programming and timing, as well as respectful good taste in creative treatment	personal privacy: bra and girdle advertisements for women, personal product advertisements for women on TV
product benefits kept in perspective in terms of normal human priorities	unrealistic product claims and implications: "floor wax, the answer to a happy home life."

The foregoing list is necessarily both general and imcomplete, for the processes of change are still proceeding at a rapid tempo.

B. Canadian Code of Advertising Standards

1. Accuracy, Clarity

Advertisements may not contain claims or statements either direct or implied which are false or misleading with regard to price, availability or performance of a product or service. Advertisers and advertising agencies must be prepared to substantiate their claims to the Council. Note that in assessing the truthfulness of a message, the Council's concern is not with the intent of the sender or the precise legality of the phrasing. Rather the focus is on the message as received or perceived, that is, the general impression conveyed by the advertisement.

2. Disguised Advertising Techniques

No advertisement shall be presented in a format which conceals its commercial intent. Advertising content, for example, should be clearly distinguished from editorial or program content. Similarly, advertisements are not acceptable if they attempt to use images or sounds of very brief duration or physically weak visual or aural techniques to convey messages below the threshold of normal human awareness. (Such messages are sometimes referred to as subliminal.)

3. Price Claims

No advertisement shall include false or misleading price claims, unrealistic price comparisons, or exaggerated claims as to worth or value. "List price," "suggested retail price," "manufacturer's list price," and "fair market value" are misleading terms when used to imply a savings unless they represent prices at which a reasonable number of the items were actually sold within the preceding six months in the market area where the advertisement appears.

163

4. Testimonials

Testimonials must reflect the genuine, reasonably current opinion of the endorser and should be based upon adequate information about, or experience with, the product or service advertised. This is not meant to preclude, however, an actor or actress presenting the true experience of an actual number of users or presenting technical information about the manufacture or testing of the product.

5. Bait and Switch

The consumer must be given a fair opportunity to purchase the goods or services offered at the terms presented. If supply of the sale item is limited, this should be mentioned in the advertisement. Refusal to show or demonstrate the product, disparagement of the advertised product by sales personnel, or demonstration of a product of superior quality, are all illustrations of the "bait and switch" technique which is a contravention of the Code.

6. Comparative Advertising

Advertisements must not discredit or attack unfairly other products, services or advertisements, or exaggerate the nature or importance of competitive differences. When comparisons are made with competing products or services, the advertiser must have substantiation available upon request from the Council.

7. Professional or Scientific Claims

Advertisements must not distort the true meaning of statements made by professionals or scientific authorities. Advertising claims must not imply they have a scientific basis they do not truly possess.

Scientific terms, technical terms, etc., should be used in general advertising only with a full sense of responsibility to the lay public.

8. Slimming, Weight Loss

Advertisements shall not state or imply that foods, food substitutes, appetite depressants, or special devices will enable a person to lose weight or girth except in conjunction with a balanced, calorie-controlled diet; and the part played by such a diet shall be given due prominence in the advertisement.

9. Guarantees

No advertisement shall offer a guarantee or warranty, unless the guarantee or warranty is fully explained as to conditions and limits, and the name of the guarantor or warrantor (is given), or it is indicated where such information may be obtained.

10. Imitation

No advertiser shall deliberately imitate the copy, slogans, or illustrations, of another advertiser in such a manner as to mislead the consumer. The accidental or unintentional use of similar or like general slogans or themes shall not be considered a contravention of this Code, but advertisers, media, and advertising agencies should be alert to the confusion that can result from such coincidences and should seek to eliminate them when discovered.

11. Safety

Advertisements shall not display a disregard for public safety or depict situations which might encourage inappropriate, unsafe or dangerous practices.

12. Exploitation of Human Misery

Advertisements may not hold out false hope in the form
of a cure or relief for the mentally or physically
handicapped, either on a temporary or permanent basis.

13. Superstition and Fears

Advertisements must not exploit the superstitious, or
play upon fears to mislead the consumer into purchasing
the advertised product or service.

14. Advertising to Children

Advertisements to children impose a special
responsibility upon the advertiser and the media. Such
advertisements should not exploit their credulity, lack
of experience, or their sense of loyalty, and should not
present information or illustrations which might result
in their physical, mental, or moral harm. (See also
Broadcast Code for Advertising to Children and the
Québec Consumer Protection Act, Bill 72.)

15. Taste, Opinion, Public Decency

a. As a public communication process, advertising
should not present demeaning or derogatory portrayals
of individuals or groups, and should not contain anything
likely, in the light of generally prevailing standards, to
cause deep or widespread offense. It is recognized, of
course, that standards of taste are subjective and vary
widely from person to person and community to
community, and are, indeed, subject to constant
change.

b. The authority of the code and the jurisdiction of the
Council are over the content of advertisements. The
code is not meant to impede in any way the sale of
products which some people, for one reason or another,

may find offensive--provided, of course, that the advertisements for such products do not contravene section a. of this Clause.

C. Advertising Industry Brief to the CRTC Task Force on Sex-Role Stereotyping

Representatives of the Canadian advertising industry, together with industries that are large users of advertising, agreed to find, through discussions within their industry associations, a plan of action they would recommend that would help resolve the problem of sex-role stereotyping in broadcast advertising.

Proceedings and hearings of the CRTC Task Force resulted in the heightening of awareness that such a problem exists. It led to the advertising industry's agreement to look at the problem, to work on resolving it, and to present a proposal that would have the backing of all sectors of the industry.

We have done so, and we are pleased to present it herewith. The views in this brief outline how the advertising industry proposes to respond to the problems that have been raised. They represent the positions of these associations: Association of Canadian Advertisers Inc.; Canadian Advertising Advisory Board; Canadian Association of Broadcasters; Canadian Cosmetic, Toiletry and Fragrance Association; Canadian Manufacturers' Association; Grocery Products Manufacturers of Canada; Institute of Canadian Advertising; Proprietary Association of Canada; Publicité-Club de Montréal; Retail Council of Canada; and the Soap and Detergent Association of Canada.

i. The Issues

All associations and the companies and people they represent agree that a number of the concerns raised by and before the Task Force require that the advertising industry change some of the ways in which women are portrayed in broadcast commercials.

Industry has made a commitment to deal with these concerns. However, industry believes that the very nature of the issue touches on judgments of the role of women in contemporary society; judgments which vary in accordance with individuals' perceptions, tastes and opinions. And because time is needed to bring about change in these attitudes and perceptions, the process is one of evolution rather than revolution.

The best of results will only be achieved if there is a raising of the consciousness of society as a whole, as well as the advertising industry, to the issues of concern to women. Although advertising accepts its responsibility to portray women and men in a manner that reflects their role in contemporary society, it does not consider that broadcast advertising should be used to promote what any groups or persons believe should be their "desired" status of women in Canada.

Where questions of taste are involved, perceptions and judgments vary, not only because of cultural and linguistic backgrounds, but also because they reflect geographic and demographic influences. To this extent, industry is firmly of the view that questions of taste and opinion cannot, and should not, as a matter of principle, be subject to regulatory intervention by governments.

The advertising industry believes that more can be accomplished if the industry itself recognizes the problem and takes on the task of dealing with it in a positive manner. Recognizing that self-imposed regulation is a difficult and serious matter, the associations submitting this brief have undertaken:

- to communicate to advertisers and the agencies preparing advertising, feminine concerns over the portrayal of women in broadcast advertising;

- to develop guidelines to help the industry present a more realistic portrayal of women in broadcast advertising;

- to establish an implementation program to stimulate a sense of commitment among advertisers and their agencies towards the elimination of any cause for legitimate concerns;

- to provide an avenue for continuing communication in relation to concerns of women or men over sex stereotyping in broadcast advertising.

ii. The Positive Portrayal of the Sexes in Broadcast Advertising

This proposal by the advertising industry recognizes two basic positions. The first is the list of concerns expressed by and before the CRTC Task Force. We see this as a clear and effective reference for identifying the spectrum of the issues raised, and it has been used as such.

The second position is that advertising is a creative medium whose purpose it is to build positive impressions in the minds of readers, viewers, or listeners, to help them remember the product or the service that is being promoted. While the advertising industry takes concerns about sex-role stereotyping into consideration, it must equally be recognized by all concerned that a number of factors and issues affect the advertising industry. It may be useful to list some of these briefly. They surround advertising like a woven fabric, each of them constituting one or more threads. None can be removed and none can be added without affecting all others.

To fulfill its purpose, advertising must function in the context of the realities of the marketplace. This means recognizing the realities of the product or service advertised, its use and its users, and seeing that the advertising reflects the constant and rapid change in the marketplace.

It means recognition of the life and lifestyles of prospects and users. It means to recognize their concerns and their ability to laugh at themselves; their creativity and living and working and relaxing; their human strengths and foibles; and, most important in this context, the human aspirations of the people addressed by the advertising in question.

The realities of the marketplace include another important set of positions. These are the existing codes of self-regulation the different segments of industry have imposed on the advertising of their products and services. It includes federal and provincial legislation, the regulations promulgated under the law.

This set of facts includes general codes of advertising standards in Canada. It includes a manual of general guidelines, a set of moral suasion which the advertising industry in Canada has imposed upon itself as a practical corollary of an ethicians' symposium summarized as "Truth in Advertising." It should be noted that truth in advertising demands both truth in the presentation of the advertised product or service, and truth in the style and manner in which it is promoted.

Advertisers live and work by ever-changing, flexible rules of taste and opinion. Within these constraints-- and the list is incomplete--the people who create advertising must do so creatively. They must use humor, information techniques, lightheartedness and seriousness, literal descriptions or fantasy--each in its place and as it may be appropriate. Appropriate, that is, not only to the advertised product or service, but even more so to the presentation and its content and, above all, to the target audience the advertiser wishes to reach.

Advertisers also recognize that individual campaigns may have desirable cumulative effects, but that the total cumulative effect of many campaigns for competing products may indeed be beyond any one advertiser's control.

It is against the background indicated here that the advertising industry proposes the following statements to be used as a basis for resolving the problem of sex-role stereotyping in advertising:

1. Advertising should recognize the changing roles of men and women in today's society and reflect the broad range of occupations for all.

2. Advertising should reflect a contemporary family structure showing men, women and children as supportive participants in home management and household tasks and equally as beneficiaries of the positive attributes of family life.

3. Advertising, in keeping with the nature of the market and the product, should reflect the wide spectrum of Canadian life portraying men and women of various ages, backgrounds and appearances, actively pursuing a wide range of interests--sports, hobbies, business--as well as home-centred activities.

4. Advertising should reflect the realities of life in terms of the intellectual and emotional equality of the sexes by showing men an women as comparably capable, resourceful, self-confident, intelligent, imaginative and independent.

5. Advertising should emphasize the positive, personal benefits derived from products or services and should avoid portraying any excessive dependence on or excessive need for them.

6. Advertising should not exploit women or men purely for attention-getting purposes. Their presence should be relevant to the advertised product.

7. Advertising should, without going to artificial extremes, employ inclusive, non-sexist terms, for example, "hours" or "working hours" rather than "man-hours"; "synthetic" rather than "man-made"; "business executives" rather than "businessmen" or "businesswomen."

8. Advertising should portray men and women as users, buyers and decision makers, both for "big-ticket" items and major services as well as smaller items.

9. Advertising should reflect a greater use of women both as voice-overs and as experts and authorities.

iii. Implementation

To ensure the effective translation of these statements into the practice of advertising on the audio-visual medium, the following program will be initiated:

1. An audio-visual presentation of the concerns about sex-role stereotyping will be prepared and

172

promoted for showing, along with appropriate guidelines, to all segments of the advertising industry to help them become aware of and understand the sex-role stereotyping problem.

2. Under the aegis of the Canadian Advertising Advisory Board, a separate Advisory Committee will be responsible for developing an effective implementation program, and for receiving and commenting on complaints related to possible continuing problems of sex-role stereotyping.

3. A continuing research program will determine the extent of the problem as described, thus creating benchmarks against which to measure problem perceptions and changes, and to provide constant control for the measurement and monitoring of change in both the perceived and actual modification of the issues.

A strategy has been completed for the audio-visual "consciousness-raising" sessions and will be presented to members of the Task Force prior to being recorded.

The need for the research project as outlined is to be found in the required substantiation, from a creative advertising standpoint, for advertisers, agencies, and commercial film producers, to find the most effective and efficient communications method to address an audience whose awareness of itself is undergoing substantive changes. The Canadian Advertising Advisory Board's special Advisory Committee is the first body of its kind specially created to deal with concerns that might still arise in the area of perceived sex-role stereotype advertising. This committee has the following terms of reference:

1. to act as the organization responsible for dissemination of the statements relating to the

portrayal of the sexes in broadcast advertising and the audio-visual presentations;

2. to provide a recognized reception point for sex-role stereotyping complaints;

3. to make appropriate observations to advertisers and their agencies, if the response from the advertiser did not either deal effectively with the complaint, or, in the view of the committee, was contrary to the spirit of the industry's own guidelines.

The members of the Advisory Committee are named by the CAAB Board of Directors. The chairman will be the chief executive officer of a significant advertiser corporation. Members include public representatives, and members from advertising agencies, broadcasters and advertisers.

iv. Conclusions

The associations subscribing to this brief have committed themselves to the principle of positive portrayal of both sexes in broadcast advertising. An Advisory Committee, set up under the Canadian Advertising Advisory Board, will direct implementation of the industry awareness program, monitor progress, and review and comment on complaints.

It is our belief that with the participation of public representatives on the CAAB Advisory Committee, this forum, rather than further government regulation or control of the advertising industry, is the most effective way of dealing with this important, complex, and sensitive issue.

APPENDIX 7

COMPLAINTS PROCEDURES AND REDRESS MECHANISMS

A. Programming Complaints

Complaints about the portrayal or presentation of women in broadcast programming can be directed either to the Canadian Association of Broadcasters, to the director of programming of the network concerned, to the station manager of the offending station, or to the CRTC. It is also recommended to bring your complaint directly to the attention of the program producer. Your complaint will be forwarded accordingly if the name of the producer, and the city where the program was produced, are noted in your letter or phone call. Complaints may be sent to one of the following addresses:

Canadian Radio-television and
Telecommunications Commission
The Secretary General
Ottawa, Ontario K1A 0N2

Canadian Association of Broadcasters
165 Sparks Street
Ottawa, Ontario K1P 5S2

Canadian Broadcasting Corporation
Louise Imbeault, Coordinator
Portrayal of Women in Programming
Box 8478
Ottawa, Ontario K1G 3J5
(613) 731-3111

CTV Television Network Ltd.
Phillip Wedge, Vice-President, Programming
42 Charles Street East
Toronto, Ontario M4Y 1T5
(416) 928-6000

Claude Blain, Executive Vice-President
TVA Television Network
Case postale 170
Succursale "C"
Suite A-762
Montréal, Québec H2L 4K3
(514) 526-9251

Bill Stewart, Vice-President, Programming
Global Television Network
81 Barber Greene Road
Don Mills, Ontario M3Z 2A2
(416) 446-5311

B. Advertising Complaints

Complaints about the portrayal or presentation of women in broadcast commercials should be forwarded to the committees listed below.

In order to facilitate the processing of complaints, it is recommended that your letter or telephone call include the name of the product, service or public service announcement objected to, as well as the date, time of day and channel on which it was broadcast.

Complaints about advertisements in print and other media are also handled by these committees:

in English:

Advisory Committee on Sex-Role Stereotyping
Advertising Advisory Board
1240 Bay Street, Suite 305
Toronto, Ontario M5R 2A7
(416) 961-6311

in French:

Le Comité consultatif sur les stéréotypes sexistes
La Confédération générale de la publicité
465 rue St-Jean
Suite 509
Montréal, Québec
H2Y 2R6

Individuals may also wish to contact the commercial acceptance departments of the networks on stations concerned. The relevant addresses are as follows:

Canadian Broadcasting Corporation
Commercial Acceptance Department
P.O. Box 500, Station "A"
Toronto, Ontario M5W 1E6
(416) 925-3311

Société Radio-Canada
Service du code publicitaire
C.P. 6000
Montréal, Québec H3C 3A8
(514) 285-3211

CTV Television Network Ltd.
Commercial Acceptance Department
42 Charles Street East
Toronto, Ontario M4Y 1T5
(416) 928-6000

Global Television Network
Commercial Acceptance Department
81 Barber Greene Road
Don Mills, Ontario M3Z 2A2
(416) 446-5311

TVA Television Network
Service du Code publicitaire
1600 est, rue de Maisonneuve
Montréal, Québec H2L 4P2
(514) 526-9251

BIBLIOGRAPHY

The following representative bibliography was compiled for use by the reader and lists books, reports, and articles on the subject of the image of women in the media.

American Association of University Women. The Image of Women in Television: A Survey and Guide. Sacramento: American Association of University Women, 1974.

Association des Femmes de Radio-Canada. Intervention at the CBC licence renewal hearing, September 1978.

Association of Canadian Advertisers. "Advertising and the Law." ACA Newsletter, 9 January 1980.

Bartos, Rena. "What Every Marketer Should Know About Women." Harvard Business Review (May-June 1978), pp. 73-85.

Bate, Barbara. "Nonsexist Language Use in Transition." Journal of Communication (Winter 1978), pp. 139-149.

Black, Hawley L. "Women as News Persons: A Look at the Role of Women Political Reporters in the Canadian Parliamentary Press Gallery." Paper presented at the Third Annual Conference of the Canadian Research Institute for the Advancement of Women, Edmonton, November 1979.

Boddewyn, J.J. "Decency and Sexism in Advertising: An International Survey of their Regulation and Self-Regulation." A report prepared for the International Advertising Association Inc., New York, December 1979.

Bodine, Ann. "Androcentrism in Prescriptive Grammar: Singular 'They,' Sex-Definite "He" and "He or She'." Language in Society, vol. 4 (1975), pp. 129-146.

Bonner, Peter. "I Dreamed I Shot a 30 in Creativity." Supplement to Marketing (Winter 1979), pp. 11-12.

Busby, Linda J. "Sex-Role Research on the Mass Media." Journal of Communication (Autumn 1975), pp. 107-131.

Butler, Matilda and Paisley, William. "Magazine Coverage of Women's Rights." Journal of Communication (Winter 1978), pp. 57-74.

_____. Women and the Media: Sourcebook for Research and Action. New York: Human Sciences Press, 1980.

CBC. Transcript: Seminar on the Portrayal of Women in CBC Programs, Ottawa, 23-23 February 1979.

_____. "The Presence, Role and Image of Women in Prime Time on the English Television Network of the CBC. An Overview." Report submitted by the Office of the Co-ordinator, Portrayal of Women, Ottawa: CBC, 1982.

_____. "The Presence, Role and Image of Women in Prime Time on the French Television Network of the CBC. An Overview." Report submitted by the Office of the Co-ordinator, Portrayal of Women, Ottawa: CBC, 1982.

Cadieux, Rita. "The Representation of Women and the Various Minorities in Broadcasting. A Question of Balance?" Paper prepared for a seminar organized by the CRTC on balance in broadcasting, Hull, Québec, 16-17 January 1981.

Canada. Royal Commission on the Status of Women. Ottawa: Queen's Printer, 1970.

Canada. Status of Women. Towards Equality for Women/Femmes en voie d'égalité. Ottawa: Supply and Services Canada, 1979.

_____. "Women in the Media." Unpublished report of the Interdepartmental Working Group on the Status of Women: Group No. 5, Communications, Ottawa: Status of Women, 1978.

Canadian Advertising Advisory Board. Women and Advertising, Today's Message--Yesterday's Images? Report of the CAAB Task Force on Women and Advertising. Toronto: CAAB, November 1977.

Canadian Teachers' Federation. Students' Name Best and Worst on Television. Ottawa: Canadian Teachers' Federation, 1980.

Cantor, Murial G. "Women and Public Broadcasting." Journal of Communication (Winter 1977), pp. 14-19.

Caron, Margaret. "The Image of Women in Canadian Television." Paper presented at the Canadian Psychological Association Meeting, Calgary, June 1980.

Collie, Ashlie and Perkins, Alana. "Women in the Media: You've Come a Long Way Baby, But..." Viewpoint Canada (November-December 1980), pp. 32-35.

Courtney, A. and Whipple, T. Canadian Perspectives on Sex Stereotyping in Advertising. Ottawa: Canadian Advisory Council on the Status of Women, 1978.

_____. "How to Portray Women in TV Commercials." Journal of Advertising Research (April 1980), pp. 53-59.

_____. Sex Stereotyping in Advertising: An Annotated Bibliography. Marketing Science Research Program Special Report. Cambridge: Marketing Science Institute, 1980.

_____. "Strategies for Self-Regulation of Sex Stereotyping in Advertising: The Canadian Experience." Paper presented at the 1978 Conference on the American Academy of Advertising, Columbia, South Carolina, April 1978.

_____. "Women in TV Commercials." Journal of Communication (Spring 1974), pp. 110-118.

Culley, James D. and Bennett, Rex. "Selling Women, Selling Blacks." Journal of Communication (Autumn 1976), pp. 160-174.

Davenport, Terry et al. The Image of Women in the Media. San Francisco: National Organization for Women (San Francisco Chapter), November 1975.

DeFleur, Melvin L. "Occupational Roles as Portrayed on Television." Public Opinion Quarterly, vol. 7 (Spring 1964), pp. 57-74.

Dohrman, Rita. "A Gender Profile of Children's Educational TV." Journal of Communication (Autumn 1975), pp. 56-65.

Dominick, Joseph R. and Rauch, G.E. "The Image of Women in Network TV Commercials." Journal of Broadcasting (Summer 1972), pp. 259-265.

Farley, Jennie. "Women's Magazines and the Equal Rights Amendments: Friend or Foe." Journal of Communication (Winter 1978), pp. 187-192.

Franzwa, Helen H. "Working Women in Fact and Fiction." Journal of Communication (Spring 1974), pp. 104-109.

Frawley, Alfred C. "Revised Expectations: A Look at the FCC's Equal Employment Opportunity Policies." Federal Communications Law Review (Summer 1980), pp. 291-313.

Fuchs, Douglas A. and Lyle, J. "Mass Media Portrayal-- Sex and Violence." Kline, Gerald F. and Tichenor, Philippe J., eds., Current Perspectives in Mass Communication Research, Beverley Hills, Calif.: Sage, 1972, pp. 235-264.

Gagnon, Lysiane et Saint-Jean, Armande. "Situation des femmes dans l'information." Paper presented at the Fédération professionnelle des journalistes du Québec, Congrès d'avril, 1977.

Gerbner, George and Signorielli, Nancy. Women and Minorities in Television Drama 1969-1978. Philadelphia: University of Pennsylvania, Annenberg School of Communications, 1979.

Goffman, Erving. Gender Advertising. New York: Harper Colphon Books, 1979.

Graham, Alma. "The Making of a Non-Sexist Dictionary." MS (December 1973), pp. 12-16.

Grills, Lee. "The Portrayal of Women on CTV." Status of Women, Ontario Advisory Council on the Status of Women (Spring 1980), p. 9.

Harris, Marjorie. "Redressing the Balance." Canadian Business (June 1981), pp. 53-61.

Haskell, Deborah. "The Depiction of Women in Leading Roles in Prime Time Television." Journal of Broadcasting (Spring 1979), pp. 191-198.

Hennesee, J.A. and Nicholson, J. "Now Says: TV Commercials Insult Women." New York Times Magazine, 20 May 1972, p. 12.

Horton, Paul B. "A Sexless Vocabulary for a Sexist Society." Intellect (December 1976), pp. 159-160.

Johnson, Carole and Kelly, Inga. "He and She: Language Fits a Changing World." Special Education in Canada (Fall 1975), pp. 8-10.

Kenny, Mary. "We Are Not All Sweet Little Dolly Birds Looking Cute." The Listener, 21 August 1980, pp. 229-230.

Klassen, Rita. "A Content Analysis of Women's Roles in TV Ads in Ontario." Undergraduate thesis, Department of Consumer Studies, University of Guelph, 1977.

Komisar, Lucy. "The Image of Women in Advertising." Gernick, Vivian and Moran, Barbara K., comp., Women in Sexist Society: Studies in Power and Powerlessness. New York: Basic Books, 1971, pp. 207-217.

Lacy, Dan. "Men's Words, Women's Roles." Saturday Review (June 1975), pp. 25-57.

Lamphier, Gary. "Stereotypes are Shown the Door." Advertising and Marketing, 14 March 1981, p. 12.

Lazer, Charles and Dier, S. "The Labor Force in Fiction." Journal of Communication (Winter 1978), pp. 174-182.

Lorimer, Rowland et al. "Consider Content: An Analysis of Two 'Canadian' Primary Language Arts Reading Series." Interchange, vol. 8, no. 4 (1977-78), pp. 64-77.

Lorimer, Rowland, and Lang, Margaret. "Sex Role Stereotyping in Elementary Readers." Interchange, vol. 20, no. 2 (1979-80), pp. 25-45.

Marecek, Jeanne et al. "Women as TV Experts: The Voice of Authority?" Journal of Communication (Winter 1978), pp. 159-168.

Martyna, Wendy. "What Does 'He' Mean? Use of the Generic Masculine." Journal of Communication (Winter 1978), pp. 130-138.

_____. "Beyond the 'He/Man' Approach: The Case for Nonsexist Language." Signs (Spring 1980), pp. 482-493.

Mayes, Sandra L. and Valentine, K.B. "Sex Role Stereotyping in Saturday Morning Cartoon Shows." Journal of Broadcasting (Winter 1979), pp. 41-50.

McDonald, Lynn. "The Silenced Majority: Women and Canadian Broadcasting." Status of Women, Ontario Advisory Council on the Status of Women (Spring 1980), pp. 2-29.

Méar, Annie. "La représentation du corps dans la publicité." Anthropologica, N.S., vol. XXI, no. 1, 1979.

_____. "L'image de la femme à la télévision: proposition d'un modèle d'analyse." Communication et information (automne 1979), pp. 102-107.

Media Report to Women. Vol. 6, no. 10, October 1978, and vol. 7, no. 9, September 1979.

Mills, Kay. "Fighting Sexism on the Airwaves." Journal of Communication (Spring 1974), pp. 150-155.

National Action Committee on the Status of Women. "The Portrayal of Women in CBC Television." Intervention to the CRTC at the CBC licence renewal hearing, September 1978.

_____. "The Portrayal of Women in CTV Television." Intervention to the CRTC at the CTV licence renewal hearing, November 1978.

National Advertising Review Board. "Advertising and Women." Report on advertising portraying or directed to women. New York: NARB, March 1975.

National Commission on the Observance of International Women's Year. Media Guidelines. L-I. Washington, D.C.: Office of Public Information, IWY Commission, 1976.

National Council of Teachers of English. "Guidelines for Non-Sexist Use of Language in NCTE Publication." Alleen Pace Nilsen, ed., Sexism and Language. Urbana, Ill.: The Council, c. 1977, pp. 181-191.

National Council on Welfare. Women and Poverty. Ottawa: The Council, 1979.

Nova Scotia Human Rights Commission. Women and Advertising. Halifax: The Commission, 1979.

O'Donnell, William J. and O'Donnell, Karen J. "Update: Sex-Role Messages in TV Commercials." Journal of Communication (Winter 1978), pp. 156-158.

Ontario Press Council. Sexism and the Newspapers. Ottawa: The Council, July 1978.

Ontario Status of Women Council. Fifth Annual Report. Toronto: The Council, 1979.

_____. "About Face: Towards a Positive Image of Women in Advertising." Report prepared by Dorothy Acton, Toronto: The Council, 1975.

Poe, Allison. "Active Women in Ads." Journal of Communication (Autumn 1976), pp. 185-192.

Purnell, Sandra E. "Politically Speaking, Do Women Exist?" Journal of Communication (Winter 1978), pp. 150-155.

Québec. Conseil du statut de la femme. L'Image des femmes dans la publicité. Préparé par Catherine Lord. Québec: le Conseil, septembre 1979.

_____. La publicité sexiste: C'est quoi? Préparé par Catherine Lord. Québec: le Conseil, octobre 1979.

"Québec Government Campaigns Against Sexist Ads." Marketing, 15 October 1979, p. 42.

Raices, Maxene. "Male and Female Roles in OECA Programming." OECA Office of Project Research, Report No. 13. Toronto: OECA, September 1976.

Rejskind, G. and Moss, B. "The Image of Women in Television Commercials." Brief presented to the Advertising Standards Council of Canada, Toronto, 1974.

Schreiber, Elliot S. "The Effects of Sex and Age on the Perceptions of TV Characters: An Inter-Age Comparison." Journal of Broadcasting (Winter 1979), pp. 81-93.

Seggar, John F., Haden, Jeffrey K., and Hannover-Gladden, Helena. "Television's Portrayal of Minorities and Women in Drama and Comedy Drama 1971-80." Journal of Broadcasting (Summer 1981), pp. 277-288.

Silverman, Theresa and Sprafkin, E.A. "Physical Contact and Sexual Behaviour on Prime-Time TV." Journal of Communication (Winter 1979), pp. 33-43.

Spender, Dale. Man Made Language. Boston: Rutledge & Kegan Paul, 1980.

Stone, Vernon A. "Attitudes Towards Television News Women." Journal of Broadcasting (Winter 1973-74), pp. 49-62.

"TV Ranked as 'Most Persuasive' and also 'Most Annoying' Ad Medium by Canadian Women." Marketing, 15 October 1979, p. 53.

Teachman, G. "The Portrayal of Canadian Cultural Diversity on Network Television." Report prepared for the Department of the Secretary of State, Multiculturalism Directorate. Toronto: PEAC Developments, 1980.

Tedesco, Nancy S. "Patterns in Prime Time." Journal of Communication (Spring 1974), pp. 119-124.

Trevelyan, Margot. "The CBC and Women: A Progress Report." Status of Women, Ontario Advisory Council on the Status of Women (Spring 1980), pp. 10-11.

Tuchman, Gaye. "Women's Depiction by the Mass Media." Signs (Spring 1979), pp. 528-542.

United States. US Commission on Civil Rights. "Window Dressing on the Set: An Update." Washington, DC: The Commission, 1979.

Warren, Denise. "Commercial Liberation." Journal of Communication (Winter 1978), pp. 160-173.

Welch, Renate L. et al. "Subtle Sex-Role Cues in Children's Commercials." Journal of Communication (Summer 1979), pp. 202-209.

Werner, Anita. "The Effects of Television on Children and Adolescents, A Case of Sex Socialization." Journal of Communication (Autumn 1975), pp. 45-50.

Wilson, S.V. Women, The Family and the Economy. Toronto: McGraw-Hill Ryerson, 1982.